BRINGING THE
CHURCH
BACK TO
CHRIST

Preparing the Bride
for the Groom's Return

Idemudia Guobadia

WESTBOW
PRESS®
A DIVISION OF THOMAS NELSON
& ZONDERVAN

WestBow Press books may be ordered through booksellers or by contacting:

WestBow Press
A Division of Thomas Nelson & Zondervan
1663 Liberty Drive
Bloomington, IN 47403
www.westbowpress.com
1 (866) 928-1240

Scripture taken from the King James Version of the Bible.

Scripture taken from the New King James Version® Copyright © 1982 by Thomas Nelson. Used by permission. All rights reserved.

Scripture quotations taken from The Holy Bible, New International Version® NIV® Copyright © 1973 1978 1984 2011 by Biblica, Inc. TM. Used by permission. All rights reserved worldwide.

Scripture taken from the NEW AMERICAN STANDARD BIBLE®, Copyright © 1960,1962,1963,1968,1971,1972,1973,1975,1977,1995 by The Lockman Foundation. Used by permission. www.Lockman.org

ISBN: 978-1-6642-0059-3 (sc)
ISBN: 978-1-6642-0060-9 (hc)
ISBN: 978-1-6642-0058-6 (e)

Library of Congress Control Number: 2020914052

Print information available on the last page.

WestBow Press rev. date: 08/17/2020

CONTENTS

ACKNOWLEDGMENTS
AND DEDICATION

Many hands and eyes were responsible for helping put this book together. I cooked the meal and they helped spice it up with salt and grace. I am indebted to them for their individual and collective efforts.

I must acknowledge my wife and partner in all things, Pastor Tayo Guobadia. Tayo works tirelessly with our children, and in making sure that the house is in order. This created a conducive atmosphere for research, thinking, and writing.

Special thanks to my mother, Florence Guobadia, for using the eyes of an eagle to scrutinize the portions of the manuscript that I assigned to her. Her thorough edits kind of reminded me of the mid-1970s when she would go over my school homework with me. Thanks mom!

I am eternally grateful to Theolyn Aimunsun, Judith Walker, Linda Grosvenor-Holland, Richard Dominique, and Jasmin Harrigan for the time they took to scrutinize and edit their assigned portions of the manuscript. Thanks to you all for the excellent quality of the finished product.

These acknowledgments will not be complete without the mention of my fellow Apostle and co-laborer in kingdom advancement, Apostle Gemma Valentine of Full Gospel Fire Deliverance Tabernacle, McKinney, Texas. Apostle Valentine, a prolific writer and author, has sacrificed precious time to cry out to God with me in intercessory and warfare prayers for the bride of Christ, mostly on Monday nights. Apostle Valentine has a burden to see the bride of Christ return to her rightful place in Christ. She has inspired me to go the extra mile.

I am so grateful to Pastor Eugene Mingo of Spoken Word of God Ministries, White Plains, New York. Pastor Eugene, thanks for all the nuggets you poured into improving the quality of this book. Thanks for the wonderful telephone conversations we had discussing the state of the

Church. You are a very sharp mind that God has used to sharpen the areas where I am rather blunt and tend to be dull.

Richard Dominique, my bosom friend, and brother in Christ for close to 25 years, you not only reviewed and edited a substantial part of this book, you also helped in stretching my thinking. For our conversations on the state of the Church and things that need to be addressed, I am so thankful. You have proven numerous times to be an encyclopedia of the Word. You are like my personal Google! Thank you.

I must also acknowledge my wonderful co-laborers in Christ at Overcomers In Christ Group of Churches that continuously demonstrate the love of Christ. Their willingness to sacrifice whatever it takes for the cause of Christ has made it so encouraging and delightful for me to serve God in their midst.

I am particularly thankful to the Holy Spirit for prompting me to write and keep on writing for rather lengthy hours on a daily basis.

Now, it gives me the utmost joy to dedicate this book to the bride of Jesus Christ, the Church, as she prepares for her meeting with her groom in the air, and the subsequent marriage supper.

Idemudia Guobadia
June 2020

INTRODUCTION

Bringing the Church Back to Christ is a book that had sat in my spirit for years. I had never thought to put it into written form. The strong urge to write this book came from the Holy Spirit as soon as I had published my sixth book, *A Deeper Walk,* in April 2020. After *A Deeper Walk* my thinking was to take a rest from writing so that I could focus on other pressing aspects of Christian ministry. The Holy Spirit had another idea. A better idea. Indeed, the wind blows where it wishes, and you hear the sound of it, but cannot tell where it comes from and where it goes. So it was when the wind of God visited me with the inspiration to write *Bringing the Church Back to Christ* as I was taking a bath in the morning of Friday May 1, 2020. The inspiration to write grew and grew, nonstop until the book was completed. Even though I have completed writing this book, I do realize that there are many more chapters needed to be written concerning this subject. I am confident that the Holy Spirit will use whoever He deems fit to write those additional chapters in one form or the other. This book, I must confess, barely scratches the surface. The purpose of this work is not to list the sins of the Church but to get believers to see the need for the Church to return to her place in Christ.

This book in your hands kind of reminds me of another book I wrote, titled *Deeper Dimensions of Power.* They were both written in a time frame of three to four weeks. With the lockdown of the coronavirus pandemic, I found myself having more time to seek God's face and to write, and I took that time by force. In the month of May 2020, I have done some light research, and articulated my thoughts on the pages of this book to convince all of the urgent need for the Church to return wholeheartedly to Christ.

The history of the Church has been a rather tumultuous but glorious one. Through the centuries the Church has had to endure persecution. Sometimes, the Church was the one persecuting others for heresy.

Sometimes, the Church acted to maintain a certain status quo that she felt was beneficial to her self-interest. The Church has been abused and has, the truth be told, also engaged in abusive behavior. The acts of the Church have not always been in accordance with the will of Christ. Christ is the Head and the Church is His body. In spite of the Church's submissive position to Christ, the Church has often acted according to her own will and in disregard to the will of her Master. For this reason, there is a need for the Church to humble herself and repent for her sinful acts. The Church must always be clothed in white, clean garments considering that she is the sole representative of Jesus Christ upon the face of the earth. Her garments have been soiled by strife, division, greed, self-interest, and a reluctance to declare truth when it mattered most. Thankfully, there is room for repentance. Thankfully, there is provision for a cleansing by the shed blood of Christ on the Cross of Calvary.

In *Bringing the Church Back to Christ*, a distinction is made between the Church as the body of Christ, and the local churches. The local churches are spread over denominations and geographical areas; and collectively, constitute the Church, the body of Christ. Christ appointed apostles, prophets, evangelists, pastors, and teachers over the local churches in order to build up the Church. The local churches tend to be institutions that are often registered by the State. They are not a creation of the government that registered them, but they must give to Caesar what belongs to Caesar. The local churches are the visible churches that the world sees. There is, however, a spiritual Church that cannot be registered by any government of the world. It is an invisible Church that is registered in the Lamb's Book of Life. So there is an invisible and a visible expression of the Church. The visible church is often seen as an institutionalized church, and as an establishment. When reference is made to organized religion, it is often made with the visible church in mind. The invisible Church, referred to as the bride of Christ or the body of Christ, is the Church that will be raptured by Christ. Members of the local churches make up the bride of Christ but not every member of the visible church is a member of the true spiritual Church, the bride of Christ.

The Church has played a prominent role in the shaping of today's world. Her role has not always been Christlike, especially in times of slavery, the Spanish inquisition, the Holocaust, Apartheid, segregation, and racism. The Church must re-examine herself (1 Corinthians 10:12, KJV), and do the needful: humble herself, turn from iniquity, and seek the face of God.

The Church being a recipient of God's grace is not appointed unto wrath. Christ is sending an end time revival to His bride. There is another wave of the Holy Spirit, and fire that is about to visit the churches. The Lord is about to visit His bride as a refiner's fire. He is coming to purge and purify His bride in anticipation of His second coming. This is the season that the Church must be on her knees in seeking the face of God. The gates are being wide-opened for the Church to come back to her redeemer, the Lord Jesus Christ.

> Therefore say to them, 'Thus says the Lord of hosts: "Return to Me," says the Lord of hosts, "and I will return to you," says the Lord of hosts. (Zechariah 1:3, NKJV).

Christ is longing to return to the Church as the Church takes steps to return to Him. His desire for the Church is more than a visitation. Christ is not content with a visit. He wants to inhabit the Church and make her His dwelling place. He does not want to have to stand outside and knock on the door to be let in. Christ desires a personal, pure, love relationship with His Church. In these end times, His word, His blood, and His fire are coming to sanctify His bride to a renewed holiness. Christ is preparing the Church to bring in an enormous harvest of souls, but the Church must first be brought back to Christ.

CHAPTER ONE

YEARNING FOR THE PLACE WHERE CHRIST IS

As the hart panteth after the water brooks, so panteth my
soul after thee, O God. My soul thirsteth for God, for the
living God: When shall I come and appear before God?
Psalm 42:1-2, KJV.

The Church is called to be at the same place where Jesus Christ is. For
the Church to get to that place, she must have an intense and deep desire
to be with God. The Church must yearn to apprehend that for which she
was apprehended for. The Church's priority must be Christ, and Christ
crucified. The Church must be constantly asking, "When shall I come and
appear before God?" The Church must never be satisfied with anything
short of the presence of God. The Church must be hungry for God.
Whatever you are hungry for the most is an indication of what you value
and cherish. Just like Moses, the Church must get to a place where she says,
'If thy presence go not with me, carry us not up hence.' (Exodus 33:15, KJV).
Just like the deer that pants for water to sustain its physical life, the believer
must pant for God to sustain his spiritual life. To stop thirsting for God is
to begin the process of dying spiritually. The Church must be connected to
Christ on all cylinders. Where there is a disconnect, there is an urgent need
for a re-connect. Where there is a spiritual thirst for God, and an intensity
of seeking after God, the Church will always be filled.

How hungry are you for God? Are you satisfied with the life that you are living? Only God can satisfy. Satisfaction will never be found in the things of this world. Besides, the things of this world are fleeting. The Church must not hunger for things that have no eternal significance. Whenever the Church has hungered or gone lusting for the things of the world, God had always considered that attitude to be adulterous. The world has a pull that can lure one away from Christ. The world is full of distractions and idols that seek to compete with God for the heart of the believer. The Church comprises of believers, and so, believers must guard their hearts against corrupting worldly influences. The pursuit of carnal things draws us farther away from God. God is a rewarder of those that diligently seek Him (Hebrews 11:6; Proverbs 8:17). The Church must be in that sacred place of intercession and prayer because that is where God can easily be found.

In bringing the Church back to Christ, we must first appreciate where Christ is and what Christ is doing through the Holy Spirit at the present time. Just as was written in the Old Testament Scriptures, Christ was born of a virgin in Bethlehem. He was baptized by John the Baptist in the wilderness and anointed of the Holy Spirit. Jesus Christ performed many signs, miracles, and wonders. He taught the people with authority. He was betrayed by one of His disciples and brought to trial before Pontius Pilate. At the insistence of His people, He was crucified on the Cross of Calvary, sandwiched between two thieves. Jesus was buried in a tomb and on the third day of His death on the Cross, He resurrected from the dead. Jesus presented Himself alive to His disciples after His resurrection by many infallible proofs, being seen by them for forty days and speaking of the things pertaining to the kingdom of God. (Acts 1:3, KJV). Shortly after instructing His disciples to wait in Jerusalem for the baptism of the Holy Spirit, Jesus Christ ascended before them into heaven. As Christ ascended, two angels confirmed that Christ will come back again in a similar manner. Christ, being God, is Omnipresent. In this sense, He is present everywhere. However, He left the earthly realm to return to heaven with the promise of sending the Holy Spirit. The promise of the Spirit was fulfilled at Pentecost. (Acts 2).

The Deity of Jesus Christ

For in him dwelleth all the fulness of the Godhead bodily. (Colossians 2:9, KJV).

Jesus saith unto him, I am the way, the truth, and the life: no man cometh unto the Father, but by me. (John 14:6, KJV).

Looking for that blessed hope, and the glorious appearing of the great God and our Savior Jesus Christ. (Titus 2:13, KJV).

[5] Let this mind be in you, which was also in Christ Jesus: [6] Who, being in the form of God, thought it not robbery to be equal with God: [7] But made himself of no reputation, and took upon him the form of a servant, and was made in the likeness of men: [8] And being found in fashion as a man, he humbled himself, and became obedient unto death, even the death of the Cross. [9] Wherefore God also hath highly exalted him, and given him a name which is above every name: [10] That at the name of Jesus every knee should bow, of things in heaven, and things in earth, and things under the earth; [11] And that every tongue should confess that Jesus Christ is Lord, to the glory of God the Father. (Philippians 2:5-11, KJV).

The Scriptures listed above, among many others, clearly reveal and establish the divinity of Jesus Christ. Jesus Christ is Lord and all the fulness of God dwells in Him. It is through Jesus Christ, the Son, that we receive eternal life. At the conclusion of Jesus' earthly ministry, He ascended into heaven to sit at the right hand of the Father where He forever makes intercession for us believers. (Romans 8:34). Jesus Christ is now our intercessor and high priest in heaven. (Hebrews 4:14-16).

Jesus as the Bridegroom and the Church as the Bride

Before He left the world, Jesus made it known to His disciples that He was going to heaven to prepare a place for us. At the moment, Jesus is in heaven preparing a place for the believers that make up His Church.

In my Father's house are many mansions, if it were not so, I would have told you. I go to prepare a place for you. And if I go and prepare a place for you, I will come again and receive you to Myself; that where I am, there you may be also. (John 14:2-3, NKJV).

Jesus is preparing a place in heaven for those that are in Christ – the new man, and not the old man. Jesus is the bridegroom and the Church is His bride. Jesus is calling on His bride to make herself ready for the marriage supper: Let us be glad and rejoice and give Him glory, for the marriage of the Lamb has come, and His wife has made herself ready. (Revelation 19:7, KJV). The essence of this book is to challenge the bride to make herself ready for the wedding supper of the bridegroom, Jesus Christ. Over the centuries, the bride (the Church) has been faced with many crises and challenges that have soiled her white garments. Time and time again, the bride has strayed away from her groom. The bride has often had little or no oil in her lamp while awaiting the bride groom. There is a Rapture that the bride is eagerly awaiting. (1 Thessalonians 4:13-18). At the Rapture, the groom will come for His bride and take her to heaven for the wedding. When the groom comes, the bride must be prepared. Not all that claim a relationship with the groom are the bride of Christ. On the appointed day of judgment, Christ will deny many that claim to have a relationship with Him. He will tell them that He never knew them. They were married to iniquity and not to Him. The Church is the bride. The bride must not flirt with sin. The bride is married to Christ. Anyone that claims to be a part of the Church of Christ and yet abides in sin is a liar. He who says, "I know Him," and does not keep His commandments, is a liar, and the truth is not in him. (1 John 2:4, KJV).

Christ is holy and commands us also to walk in holiness before Him. (1 Peter 1:15-16). God is calling now for all to repent and live in holiness. Without holiness no man will see God. God is not willing that any man should perish. Rather, God wants all men to come to repentance. Holiness enables us to fellowship with God. Those that mention the name of Christ must depart from iniquity. In getting ready, the Church must cleanse herself from iniquity and pursue righteousness. The Church, as an institution, has had her share of participating in iniquities from the times of slavery to these times of merchandizing the gospel. The Lord knows those in the local churches that are His. It is those that are truly in Christ that constitute the body of Christ. The ones that are in Christ are the bride of Christ - the Church.

If Jesus Christ were to come today, will the Church be prepared? This question has laid a heavy burden on my heart especially as quite a number of local churches have shut their doors to the Spirit of Christ. What has happened to the Church from the time of Pentecost until now? Where did the Church begin to stray? At what point did the Church start deviating from the teachings of Jesus Christ that are embedded in the Holy Bible? Can the Church return to her first love before her lampstand is removed from its place? Who will rescue the Church?

The answer to these questions will be found in the Church humbling herself. God calls on His people in 2 Chronicles 7:14 to humble themselves, and pray, and seek His face. He tells His people to turn from their wicked ways. In other words, they must not continue on their path of wickedness. They must repent. Only then will God hear the cry of His people from heaven and forgive their sins. The Church must return to the teachings of the Cross of Christ. We cannot love Christ and in the same vein, be an enemy of the Cross of Christ. (Philippians 3:18). The Church of the living God must no longer set her mind on earthly things. We must always remember that our citizenship is in heaven, from which we also eagerly wait for the Savior, the Lord Jesus Christ. (Philippians 3:19-20). As a result of the sins of mankind, *and the Church is not exempt*, the land today is in urgent need of healing. Revival will bring a healing to the land.

But then again, who will rescue the Church? Who will lead the Church to returning to the place where Christ is and has always been? The answer was provided by Jesus Christ as He prepared His bride for His departure. He told His bride that He will send her another Comforter, the Spirit of Truth - the Holy Spirit. Many times, the bride has grieved the Holy Spirit and sought to quench the Spirit's fire. In some churches, the person, the gifts, and the authority of the Holy Spirit have been denied. Like in Acts 19, some churches are carrying on as if they have not even heard of the Holy Spirit. Every time the Church shut out the Holy Spirit from her business, the business of the Church was carried out by the spirit of man, and the spirit of the world. When churches refuse to be led by the Holy Spirit, they will be led by a spirit of error, which is a spirit directly from Satan. For righteousness and order to prevail, all agents of Satan must be cast out of our local churches. History has shown that whenever the Holy Spirit was not in the driver's seat, the bride drifted and strayed into things that did not please her bridegroom. But the bridegroom is patient and longsuffering. This bridegroom loves His bride unconditionally and gave Himself up to redeem her with His blood. In these last days, the bridegroom is going to purge and prune His bride by fire to make sure she is ready when the trumpet sounds. The bridegroom is the One that baptizes with the Holy Spirit, and fire. (Luke 3:16).

Time is running out. These are the last days and the bride has to be ready. The bride will be made ready just as the five wise virgins were ready to meet their bridegroom in Matthew 25. The task of getting the bride ready is not one that is for man alone. And *to her it was granted* to be arrayed in fine linen, clean and bright, for the fine linen is the righteous acts of the saints. (Revelation 19:8, KJV). (Emphasis in italics, mine.) It is going to take an extraordinary work of grace to get the bride ready to meet the One that paid the bride price and that is coming back for her. Before the bridegroom returns for His bride, the bride needs to return to the bridegroom in Spirit and in Truth.

To get the bride prepared is going to take enormous spiritual warfare against gargantuan forces from the pit of hell. Now that the bridegroom has tarried in coming, the bride is going to have to fast and pray like she never did before. There is a war to be fought against principalities and powers, the rulers of darkness of this world, and spiritual wickedness in high places. The war must be continuously fought to stop Satan from polluting the bride and accusing her of being dressed in filthy garments. (Zechariah 3:1-3). The war must be fought to overthrow hindering forces of darkness standing in the way of the gospel being preached in all the earth. The Church, being at the forefront of advancing the kingdom of God on earth, is going to have to take all things pertaining to the kingdom by force. Christ has given the Church the victory but there are still battles to be fought and won on this side of eternity. There are prizes and crowns to be won at the judgment seat of Christ. The present day Church is overdue for a radical, biblical, spiritual transformation. The bride's light needs to shine in the darkness. The bride must realize that she has no light of her own. She must take the light of Christ and be willing to be examined by that light before she beams it on a lost and dying world. It is by the Word of God, which is the light of God, that we see where the Church has fallen and needs to get back on her feet. Only the light of God can show us the true state of affairs of the Church. Christ is the life of the Church. It is in Christ that we live, and move, and have our being. (Acts 17:28).

The bride has been raised up together *with* Christ, and made to sit together *in* Christ in the heavenly places. (Ephesians 2:6, KJV: emphasis in italics are mine). This is where the bride must always be: in Christ and with Christ. To be *with* Christ means that we must be on the same side with Him. We must agree with Him. We must be helping Him gather or else, we are scattering. To be *in* Christ is to have taken up a new identity whereby our old nature has passed, and given way to the new creation. The Church is appointed to be in Christ and with Christ.

Usurpers of the Bridegroom

There is a growing tendency in certain parts of Christendom to elevate pastors and other leaders to the position of the bridegroom, Jesus Christ. The pastor is given so much attention and Jesus is placed at the periphery. The pastor, in some cases, has become the star of the show. The name of Jesus Christ has been relegated to an afterthought. The name of Jesus is mentioned on occasion but, the glory is put on the pastor or other leader in a subtle manner. The church in Corinth experienced this issue. Some claimed to be of Paul, and some of Apollos. (1 Corinthians 3:4-5). The believer's identity in Christ is not based on any man. It is based on the finished work of Christ on the Cross of Calvary. These days many believers are members of a local church because of the person or giftings of the pastor and not necessarily because the Spirit of God led them there. When believers put their attention on a man and make him their idol, God is displeased. Apostle Paul made the Corinthian church aware that their engaging in this practice made them carnal, and not spiritual. This is why sometimes, when a leader leaves a church, many people follow him. This gives the impression that they were not in that church for Jesus but, for a man.

When man is elevated instead of Christ, the Holy Spirit is grieved. Eventually, the Holy Spirit may depart from that church unannounced. When the Holy Spirit came to the Church in Acts 2, He came announced as a rushing mighty wind. However, when He leaves, He often leaves quietly. The affected church would still be engaged in church activities and may not even realize that the Holy Spirit has departed from them. A religious spirit is often quick to fill the vacuum created by the departure of the Holy Spirit. Men that usurp the glory that belong to Christ are often the ones that never open the door for Christ to come in.

When God does wonders in the congregation of His people, the best appreciation we can give to God is to give Him all the glory. God takes

His glory very seriously and will not share it with any man. The practice of church websites and other social media platforms engaging in self-promotion of men of God is one example, among several, God being robbed of His glory. Our websites and social media space should be used to glorify Jesus Christ and not to give praise to a church or a man. When a church is known more for being a church or for having a particular pastor, that church has failed to make Christ known in His fullest. Christ must always be at the center of all that we say and do.

The Church must ensure that she deflects the glory and attention of herself and puts it on Christ. The Bible tells us to be moderate in all things. Let your moderation be known to all men. The Lord is at hand. (Philippians 4:5, KJV). Men of God that live flamboyant and celebrity lifestyles place undue attention on themselves that ought to be placed on Jesus. For the Church to be at the place where Christ is, and to yearn for that place, there must be humility. Pride always steals God's glory. Pride is a glory thief. Pride says, "I did it." Pride says, "Without me, it could not have been done." Pride loves praise from men. Pride feels entitled to a part of God's glory. It is not only individuals that are subject to pride. Pride can be in a nation, an institution, and in a church. A church can be prideful and thus, misappropriate the glory of God for her benefit. God resists the proud but gives grace unto the humble. (James 4:6, KJV). If we humble ourselves in the sight of the Lord, He shall lift us up. (James 4:10, KJV). A church that misappropriates God's glory in order to lure people into her fold runs the risk of grieving the Holy Spirit. Christ is not pleased with the spirit of competition among churches. Christ wants to see churches work in unity and in partnership. Competition makes churches see each other as rivals rather than as members of the same body. Churches must see each other as working for the same Lord. Some churches within the same geographical area have been known to quarrel over membership. Competition among churches breeds an unhealthy rivalry. The competitive spirit always seduces its victim to engage in self-promotion in order to 'win.' In this case, the opposite will be the case. What a church 'gains' by using a spirit of competition, is actually nothing but a loss. Gain, apart from Christ, is nothing. 'But what things were gain to me, those I counted loss for Christ.' (Philippians 3:7, KJV).

In 2 Kings 20, Hezekiah had recovered from a sickness that was initially unto death. The king of Babylon sent men to Hezekiah, presumably to encourage him regarding his sickness. Rather than tell the messengers from Babylon how God had healed him, king Hezekiah showed them all his wealth and treasures. Hezekiah by his actions showed that he wanted to be admired for what he had. By placing the focus on himself, Hezekiah missed the opportunity to give God the glory for all that God had done in his life. Hezekiah's action incurred heavy consequences from God. Churches can learn a lesson from this story. The lesson to learn here is modesty. When the Church truly yearns to be at the place where Christ is, she will make the necessary adjustments to do the things that please Christ. Christ is in a holy place and we cannot approach that place with even an iota of carnality.

The Place of Fellowship

Christ is the source and sustainer of life for the Church. The Church must be constantly connected to Christ in fellowship, otherwise, she will become stale, and then eventually, decay. Christ vowed never to leave nor forsake the Church. The true Church of Christ will always be connected to Christ through the Word of God and by the Holy Spirit. The Church's relationship with Christ is based on love. Christ demonstrated His love for the Church by dying for her. The Church demonstrates her love for Christ by living for Him. The Church is called into fellowship with Christ. This fellowship is a deep communion with Christ. It is the kind of fellowship that admits of no rival fellowship.

> [38] Now it came to pass, as they went, that he entered into a certain village: and a certain woman named Martha received him into her house. [39] And she had a sister called Mary, which also sat at Jesus' feet, and heard his word. [40] But Martha was cumbered about much serving, and came to him, and said, Lord, dost thou not care that my sister hath left me to serve alone? bid her therefore that she help me. [41] And Jesus answered and said unto her, Martha, Martha, thou art careful and troubled about many things: [42] But one thing is needful: and Mary hath chosen that good part, which shall not be taken away from her. (Luke 10:38-42, KJV).

The Church has a few lessons to learn from the story of these two sisters: Mary and Martha. Jesus paid a visit to the home of Mary and

Martha. Martha kept busy with much serving. Martha was distracted by matters which in light of Jesus' visit, should not have been given priority. Mary, rather than seek a reputation as a good housekeeper, sought to be at the feet of Christ and grow as a disciple of Christ. Martha became upset with Mary because Mary was not assisting her with the housework needed to serve Jesus. Mary was busy hanging out with Jesus. Sometimes, the Church, just like Martha, gets so bogged down by activities, including activities relating to the Kingdom of God. The Church needs to get to the place of Mary and just sit at Jesus' feet. Martha, being upset with Mary, instead of talking directly to Mary, goes directly to Jesus to complain. Martha was soliciting support from Jesus. Jesus corrected Martha. In the same way, Jesus wants to bring correction to the Church. Jesus wants to get the Church back to that place of true fellowship with Him. Worshippers do not complain. Mary was a worshipper. Worship could also be a listening experience that increases our understanding of Who God is. As Mary listened to Jesus, she was learning of Him. Mary chose to fellowship with Jesus. Fellowship with Christ takes priority over other matters. The Church needs to get back to the place where it is all about Jesus. Jesus is waiting for the Church to come back to her rightful place: at His feet.

CHAPTER TWO

THE AGE OF THE CHURCH

"When our Lord and Master Jesus Christ
said, 'Repent,' He meant that the entire life of
believers should be a life of repentance."
Martin Luther, The Ninety-Five Theses

Identifying Christ

The prophets of the Old Testament had rightly prophesied the coming of
the Messiah, how he would be identified, and His mission. Jesus Christ
fulfilled all the Old Testament prophecies, many of which were written
centuries prior to His birth. Jesus is the Christ, the Anointed One, the
Messiah. In Isaiah 7:14, KJV, the Prophet Isaiah had written that the Lord
shall give a sign by a virgin conceiving and bearing a son, and His name
shall be Immanuel. In Luke 1, the angel Gabriel was sent from God to a
young virgin, Mary. The angel informed Mary that she would conceive in
her womb and bring forth a son, and shall call Him, Jesus. Mary questioned
the angel about this by asserting her virginity. Matthew 1:18 records the
birth of Jesus by narrating that Mary the mother of Jesus was espoused to
Joseph, and bore Jesus before she and Joseph consummated their marriage.
Jesus is the only one that has fulfilled the prophecy of being born of a
virgin.

Again in Isaiah 11:2 and Isaiah 42:1, it was prophesied that the Spirit of
the Lord would rest on Christ. God the Father promised to put His Spirit

upon Christ. In Isaiah 61:1, Isaiah testifies that the Spirit of the Lord will be upon Christ because He had been appointed to preach good news to the poor. We see Jesus fulfilling these prophecies in the New Testament. Matthew 3:16 records how as soon as Jesus was baptized, He went up out of the water. At that moment heaven was opened, and the Spirit of God descended upon Him like a dove.

In Psalm 110:4 it was prophesied that Christ will function as a high priest forever, in the order of Melchizedek. The writings in the New Testament book of Hebrews Chapters 6 through 9 confirm Jesus' priestly role in the order of Melchizedek. We see Jesus Christ performing this priestly role in Luke 23:34 when He asks His father to forgive the people for not knowing what they were doing.

The intent of this book is not to prove that Jesus is the Christ. This is taken as a given considering that only Jesus fulfilled all the requirements of the Old Testament prophecies. Besides, sometimes, when there was uncertainty as to who Jesus really was, Jesus took the opportunity to reveal Himself as the Messiah. As we shall see, throughout the course of Jesus' earthly ministry, He took the time to assert and confirm who He is.

In Matthew 16, Jesus had questioned His disciples regarding who men though that He was. They reported to Him that some thought He was Elijah, and others thought He was Jeremiah or John the Baptist or some other great prophet. At this point in their conversation, Jesus asked His disciples who they thought that He was. Simon Peter answered that Jesus was the Christ, the Son of the living God. The Bible records Jesus' response to Peter's answer as follows:

> And Jesus answered and said unto him, blessed art thou, Simon Barjona: for flesh and blood hath not revealed it unto thee, but my Father which is in heaven. And I say unto thee, that thou art Peter, and upon this rock I will build my church; and the gates of hell shall not prevail against it ... Then charged he his disciples that they should tell no man that he was Jesus the Christ. (Matthew 16:17-18, 20, KJV).

Here, in Matthew 16:20, Jesus validates the revelation given to Simon Peter that He, Jesus is Christ. Furthermore, in the book of Revelation, Jesus introduces Himself as follows:

> I am Alpha and Omega, the beginning and the ending, saith the Lord, which is, and which was, and which is to come, the Almighty. (Revelation 1:8, KJV).

> And to the angel of the church in Philadelphia write; These things saith he that is holy, he that is true, he that hath the key of David, he that openeth, and no man shutteth; and shutteth, and no man openeth. (Revelation 3:7, KJV).

In Revelation 19, we see the resurrected Jesus Christ leading the armies of heaven to make war against the beast and the false prophet. Here, Jesus is clothed with a vesture dipped in blood: and His name is called the Word of God. In addition, on His vesture and thigh is a name written: KING OF KINGS, AND LORD OF LORDS. Jesus' name being the Word of God reveals Him as God. In John 1:1, the Word of God is revealed as God. In John 1:14, we see that the Word of God became flesh and dwelt with man while endued with the glory of the Father and full of grace and truth. Furthermore, Jesus bearing the name of King of kings, and Lord of lords reveals Him as Sovereign.

> Therefore let all the house of Israel know assuredly, that God hath made that same Jesus, whom ye have crucified, both Lord and Christ. (Acts 2:36, KJV).

Knowing who Jesus is becomes pivotal in evaluating the need of the Church to return back to her rightful place in Christ. Jesus is the One building His Church and He has said that the gates of hell shall not prevail against the Church. The gates of hell are doing all they can to drive the Church farther away from Christ by the use of temptation, deception, distraction, compromise, and other stratagem to undermine the Church's relationship with Christ. The gates of hell shall not prevail in its quest to infiltrate, undermine, intimidate, and dominate the Church. Christ is the One building the Church and He has said that the gates of hell would not be allowed to get the upper hand and prevail. This bring us to the question of what or who really is the Church that Christ is building.

There is the Church which is the whole, universal, and entire body of Christ. There are also local churches which, though differing from one another, may constitute the Church of Christ. The local churches are the visible expression of the body of Christ. The invisible Church is the true spiritual body of Christ.

The Church that Jesus Christ is Building

From the foundation of the world, the plan of redemption had always been that Jesus Christ the Son will reconcile sinful man back to God. Redeemed man in Christ is in a relationship with Jesus Christ that can be described as that of bride and bridegroom.

> For as a young man marrieth a virgin, So shall thy sons marry thee: And as the bridegroom rejoiceth over the bride, so shall thy God rejoice over thee. (Isaiah 62:5, KJV).

Jesus is building a Church that is connected to Him by intimate relationship, just as a bride is connected to the bridegroom. The Church is the bride of Christ. Christ knows His bride and will never be fooled by a counterfeit bride. Because a body is labelled as a church does not necessarily mean that it is a church that Christ is building or a church that He recognizes. Christ's Church flows from Christ and is sustained by Christ. The Church of Christ lives and moves and has her being in Christ (Acts 17:28). Many institutions created by organized religion have carried out their work under the label of a church name. This, as we shall see, does not necessarily make that institution a church. The real Church is not an institution: rather, she is a spiritual community of believers.

The bride of Christ is also known as the body of Christ. Christ is the head of this body. "And God placed all things under his feet and appointed him to be head over everything for the church, which is his body, the fullness of him who fills everything in every way." (Ephesians 1:22-23, NIV). Concerning this body, the Church, Jesus said:

> And other sheep I have, which are not of this fold: them also I must bring, and they shall hear my voice; and there shall be one fold, and one shepherd. John 10:16, KJV.

The Church that Christ is building is designed not only to be in a harmonious relationship with Christ, but also, to be in such a harmonious relationship within herself. The Church is one flock, one-fold, under one shepherd: our Lord and Savior Jesus Christ. The Church that Christ told Simon Peter in Matthew 16:18 that He will build is a church that is connected to Him. Jesus is the true vine and the body of Christ - the congregation of believers - are the branches. A church that is not connected to Christ is not a church belonging to Christ. The Church must be connected to Christ by faith, by the Word of God, by the Spirit of God, and by obedience. The Apostle Paul in his second epistle to the church in Corinth mentioned how he was jealous for that church with a godly jealousy and how he had promised them to one husband, to Christ, as a chaste virgin. (2 Corinthians 11:2, kjv). It follows that the Church is comprised of individuals who by faith have accepted Jesus Christ as their Lord and Savior. (John 1:12). The Church consists of true believers in Christ, and not denominations. Many organizations, in the course of history, that have claimed church status, are probably not even recognized by Christ as His Church. These are impostor churches. These are pseudo-churches acting as angels of light. They may even be of a synagogue of Satan (Revelation 2:9).

For the Church to find her rightful place in Christ, we believers must begin to appreciate that the Church is not a work of man. She is a work and a creation of God. The Church was established in the person and work of Christ to fulfill God's eternal purpose. When Christ ascended into heaven, He sent down the Holy Spirit to His body to comfort, lead, and empower His body. The real Church has the Spirit of Christ, the Holy Spirit, flowing through her. For if any man hath not the Spirit of Christ, he is not of Christ. For as many as are led by the Spirit of God, they are the sons of God. (Romans 8:9, 14).

Today, there are multiple problems confronting the Church that have caused many local churches to deviate from the original plan of God. For us to appreciate the enormity of the challenges and responsibilities before the Church, it is prudent to briefly review the history of the Church in broad terms to see, how the Church arrived at her current state today.

The Birthing of the Church

The church age refers to the period when the Church came into being at Pentecost (Acts 2) and up until the time when the Church will be raptured (1 Thessalonians 4:13-17; 1 Thessalonians 5:9). In other words, the church age represents the period of time that the Church, the true bride of Christ, is on earth. When the Church is taken away, many local churches will be left behind. The Rapture of the Church will clearly show the distinction between the Church and many of the institutionalized local churches that are not recognized by Christ.

Faith preceded the birthing of the Church. Before Pentecost, faith existed. Faith waited for Pentecost. Christian faith existed right from the time followers of Jesus began to believe that He was the Messiah. This Christian faith faced its greatest challenge on a weekend. It was confirmed on a weekend between Good Friday and Resurrection Sunday. In a sense, today, faith is still being established somewhere between Good Friday and Resurrection Sunday. In the course of our Christian journey, we eventually get to our own Good Friday. On Good Friday, we experience a traumatic dying that requires that we be bold and courageous. Friday represents a sort of demolition. On Saturday, there is a waiting. Faith waits amidst the silence of the Saturday between Good Friday and Resurrection Sunday. That Saturday is the day of waiting after going through the trials and losses of Friday. Saturday calls for reflection. Faith reflects on the substance of things hoped for. Our faith was established on Resurrection Sunday. Having gone through the ordeal of Good Friday that required us to die to ourselves, we lost our very carnality. Crucifixion strips us of our carnality. While our flesh experienced crucifixion, our faith reflected on the promise of Sunday morning without quite seeing it yet. By Resurrection Sunday, our common faith was confirmed to be a living faith. Faith had endured but the Church was yet to be born. With faith preceding it, the Church was born at Pentecost.

Until the Church is taken away from the earth by the Rapture, the earth remains under a dispensation of grace. The law was given by Moses, but grace and truth came by Jesus Christ. (John 1:17). Christ the bridegroom and head of the body, is eternal. The Church, the bride and body of Christ on the other hand, is not eternal but is promised eternal life. In Matthew 16:18, Jesus promised that He will build His Church. He has kept that promise and the Church of Christ was birthed by the Holy Spirit on the day of Pentecost. The church age is evident by, and sealed with, the Holy Spirit's indwelling of members of the body of Christ.

The age of the church is traced from when the early believers gathered by faith in Jerusalem to wait for the promise of the Father as Christ instructed. In Acts 1, Jesus after resurrecting from the dead with many infallible proofs, commanded His disciples as they were gathered together, not to depart from Jerusalem but to wait for the promise of the Holy Spirit. Jesus wanted His disciples to do nothing until they were baptized with the Holy Spirit. They were to wait in Jerusalem where God had chosen to place His name. (2 Chronicles 6:6). It was at Jerusalem that the Holy Spirit, as prophesied by the Prophet Joel in Joel 2:28-32, came down from heaven to quicken the assembled body of believers with the breath and fire of Christ.

The disciples of Jesus, prior to His ascension, consisted of ordinary men and women, few of whom had a formal education. Jesus' resurrection confirmed His deity and so these disciples of Jesus were not willing to disperse though their shepherd was struck. The smitten shepherd that died on the Cross was now alive forevermore and had re-gathered His scattered flock back to Himself in Jerusalem. Thus, Jesus was not viewed among His followers as some great leader whose body was decomposing in a grave. He was rightly viewed as a leader with deity that had defied death. Jesus confirmed His lordship to all that would believe by rising from the dead. For this singular reason, it became easy for His disciples to wait in Jerusalem as He had instructed.

In Acts 2, it is recorded how on the day of Pentecost, the Holy Spirit came as a rushing mighty wind from heaven and filled the house where all the disciples were. Cloven tongues as of fire sat upon each of them and they were all filled with the Holy Spirit. They began to speak with other tongues as the Spirit gave them utterance. It was at this point in time, that the prophecy of Joel 2:28-29 was fulfilled that God will pour out His Spirit upon all flesh. It was this baptism of the Holy Spirit that brought about the believers being baptized into one body (the Church).

> For by one Spirit are we all baptized into one body, whether we be Jews or Gentiles, whether we be bond or free; and have been all made to drink into one Spirit. (1 Corinthians 12:13, KJV).

It was this outpouring of the Holy Spirit at Pentecost that baptized the tarrying believers, that waited and assembled in Jerusalem, into one body. This one body refers to the body of Christ, known as the Church. This is how (through the Holy Spirit), when (at Pentecost), and where (in Jerusalem) the Church was born. The early Church grew out of an environment in Jerusalem that was heavily influenced by the dominant Jewish, Roman, and Greek culture of the day. These dominant cultures were to varying degrees, opposed to the Church and its progress. Rome, unlike the Jewish authorities, allowed Israel a good measure of religious freedom. The Jewish Sanhedrin that sat at Jerusalem consisted of the high priest that presided and seventy other elders. The Sanhedrin was recognized by Rome as having religious authority over Jewish affairs. While this Sanhedrin sought to truncate the growth of the early Church; Rome to a larger extent, appeared neutral. Rome, the dominant political power at the time that Israel was subject to, was often reluctant to get involved in Jewish religious rivalries. In the first century when the Church came on the scene, from the onset, it had to contend with the animosity of Judaism that was spearheaded by the Pharisees and Sadducees. It would seem like the newly birthed Church had no chance of survival against the forces arrayed against it. How would mere men, some fishermen with no political influence measure up and build the Church in such a hostile environment? Jesus understood this challenge, and for this reason, told His disciples to wait for the empowerment of the Holy Spirit in Jerusalem. They would be empowered by the Holy Spirit to advance the cause of Christ in the midst of heavy opposition. The Church was empowered by the Holy Spirit to overcome the gates of hell.

The early Church, that was birthed in Jerusalem, exercised its God-given power in the name of Jesus Christ. This was at a time when Caesar of Rome was likened unto a god. During that time period, it was common to say, "In the name of Caesar." By saying, "In the name of Jesus," the early disciples were seen as equating the authority of Jesus to that of Caesar and even above it. As far as the early Church was concerned, and in accordance with the Scriptures, the name of Jesus bestowed dominion over every other power. All powers of hell are subject to the name of Jesus. This new faith in Christ ran the risk of violating many of the societal norms of the times.

Persecution Against the Early Church

Within a short time after Pentecost, the early churches had recorded remarkable successes. In Acts 2:41, about three thousand souls were added to the Church. This was no surprise as the Church continued steadfastly in the Apostles' doctrine and fellowship, in the breaking of bread, and in prayers. As they continued daily with one accord in the temple and praising God, they had favor with all the people. The Lord daily added such as should be saved. The remarkable growth of the Church was followed by the miraculous healing of a lame man in Acts 3. This miracle, that Christ did through the hands of Peter and John, stirred up the city and brought more attention to the name of Jesus. This in turn, led to an additional five thousand men being saved (Acts 4:4). As a result, Peter and John were arrested and this marked the beginning of the persecution of the churches. The Jewish religious authorities - consisting of the priests, captain of the temple, and the Sadducees - detained Peter and John and brought them to trial the following day before the high priest, their rulers, the elders, and scribes. For the very first time, the Church was on trial with Peter and John in the dock. The sitting council admitted among themselves that a notable miracle had been done by Peter and John and that it could not be denied. They threatened Peter and John not to speak at all nor teach any more in the name of Jesus. "But Peter and John answered and said unto them, Whether it be right in the sight of God to hearken unto you more than unto God, judge ye. For we cannot but speak the things which we have seen and heard." (Acts 4:19-20, KJV). This was how the early Church responded to persecution and threats. They remained faithful to Christ even in the midst of grave peril.

As time progressed, the disciples of Christ faced more persecution with the imprisonment of the apostles, but God sent an angel to deliver them. (Acts 5:17-19). In Acts 7, Stephen was stoned to death for preaching the gospel and holding on to his faith in Christ. By Acts 8, a great persecution broke out against the church which was at Jerusalem. This great persecution caused the Jerusalem church to be scattered abroad, except the apostles. In spite of the persecution, the apostles remained in Jerusalem. The apostles were fearless and unequivocally demonstrated a willingness to contend for the faith even at the expense of their lives. The history of the early Church was characterized by persecution in the form of execution of the faithful, martyrdoms, imprisonment of the church leaders, beatings, threats, hunting down, uproars, and violent rejections from certain towns and communities. Interestingly, the persecution that caused the early Church to be scattered abroad, was also the means by which the Christian faith spread to diverse places abroad. What Satan meant for evil, God used for good by advancing the cause of Christ.

The Rise of Constantine and the Council of Nicaea

Prior to Constantine assuming the emperorship of Rome, there was what was known as The Great Persecution that encouraged such violent animosity against Christians by AD 304. It was common throughout most parts of the vast Roman Empire to offer public sacrifices and libations to idols or risk the penalty of death. Christians had their properties confiscated, bishops were ordered to be arrested, and believers were stripped of their social status. In this time period, many Christians were harassed and martyred. Many Christian places of worship were destroyed. There was a determined effort to crush Christianity by all means. Hatred of Christians increased. Many were put to death by beheading, by being thrown to lions and other wild beasts, or by being burnt alive in fire. Such was the fate of the Church prior to the rise of Constantine in about AD 312. Emperor Constantine attributed his military victories, especially the one that consolidated his power, not to the pagan gods of Rome, but to Christ. Constantine claimed to have seen a vision of a Cross of light prior to fighting the battle that brought him to power. Not surprising, emperor Constantine decreed that the persecution of Christians should cease. He was also known to give generous financial support to advancing the cause of Christ. Constantine was responsible for facilitating the restoration of confiscated Church lands and properties, including those belonging to individual Christians. During the reign of Emperor Constantine, there was a good measure of religious freedom and less persecution of Christians. By adopting Christianity as the official religion of Rome, Constantine was able to appropriate the churches to himself while giving the churches some privileges. So in exchange for societal privileges, it seemed like the Church was used in conferring some legitimacy upon the Emperor Constantine. The question remains as to who used whom. Did the churches use Constantine? Or did Constantine use the churches to consolidate his hold on Rome?

Some historians still raise doubts about the sincerity of Constantine's faith in Christ considering that he also supported some pagan religions. He did not relinquish some of his pagan titles associated with his emperorship and allowed pagan rites to continue alongside Christianity. Nonetheless, it was Emperor Constantine that convened the famous Council of Nicaea in AD 325. The Council of Nicaea - consisting of 300 Bishops - sought to address doctrinal disputes within the Church, especially as relating to the deity of Jesus Christ and the Trinity. These disputes were tearing the

Church apart and Constantine sought to reconcile the opposing viewpoints within the Church. Emperor Constantine charged the Council of Bishops to resolve these issues by a majority vote. However, the Nicaean Council of Bishops resolved these doctrinal questions by relying solely on the Bible and with an overwhelming majority resolved, among other things, that the deity of Christ was unquestionable and represented the accepted position of the Church. Christ was stated to be co-equal and co-eternal with the Father. This position of the Council of Nicaea became known as the Nicene Creed.

At the Council of Nicaea, it would appear that God used a secular emperor to authoritatively pronounce and establish Biblical doctrine in the Church by the 4th century. The unintended effect of the Council of Nicaea however was that it gave the government the leeway to interfere in ecclesiastical matters. Subsequently, other Councils met at Nicene to resolve other doctrinal issues and church matters. This has led some, in the modern churches, to question the motive and authority behind these meetings. However, the first Nicene Council of AD 325 merely adopted the position of the Bible as the governing authority for the Church. This was a major breakthrough for the Church that constantly faced harassment, extreme persecution, and fragmentation, fueled by conflicts over doctrine. By the affirmation of the deity of Jesus Christ, at the Council of Nicaea, the Church had been brought closer to Christ.

The Church in the Era of Slavery and the Slave Trade

In bringing the Church back to Christ, we must examine the role of the Church in the institution of slavery.

The consequences of slavery are still being felt in our societies. These include racism, hatred, anger, mistrust, prejudices, among others. Prior to the earthly ministry of Jesus Christ, slavery had been an institution that existed in many societies. Slavery continued centuries after Christ completed His earthly ministry and established His Church

> And which of you, having a servant plowing or tending sheep, will say to him when he has come in from the field, 'Come at once and sit down to eat'? But will he not rather say to him, 'Prepare something for my supper, and gird

yourself and serve me till I have eaten and drunk, and afterward you will eat and drink'? Does he thank that servant because he did the things that were commanded him? I think not. So likewise you, when you have done all those things which you are commanded, say, 'We are unprofitable servants. We have done what was our duty to do." (Luke 17:7-10, NKJV).

In Luke 17:7-10, Jesus is teaching us that a faithful servant attends to his duties first, and then to himself afterwards. The faithful servant merely did what was his duty to do and so in essence, was no better than an unprofitable servant. Through this teaching, Jesus is showing us that salvation by works has no place in the kingdom. At this point, it is left for the master to say to the servant, "well done, good and faithful servant." (Matthew 25:21, KJV). The servant referred to by Christ in Luke 17 is one that is a slave, as opposed to a freeman. Older versions of the King James version use the term, 'slave.' It almost seems as if the word, 'slave' was deliberately lost in subsequent translations to do away with the stigma attached to slavery and the gross injustices inflicted on mankind by the institution of slavery. To the credit of the New American Standard Bible (NASB), the word "slave" is used in Luke 17. Substantial differences exist between a servant and a slave. Servants are hired; whereas slaves are owned. Servants can choose whom they work for. A slave does not have that freedom of choice: he has no will of his own. Strict obedience and devotion to his master is required of him at all times. He must attend to the needs, wishes, and wants of his master. He is an unprofitable bondservant, a slave that can claim no merit. He is not worthy and has no worth apart from waiting upon his master. This can be somewhat likened to the true followers and worshippers of God.

The gospel radically changes who we are. In Christ, we are a new creation and so whether slave or free, we have been set free from sin. However, because Jesus bought us with a price - His redeeming blood - we have become slaves to Him. The Church represents a congregation of slaves that are owned by Christ. It is for this reason that we must be fully yielded to Christ. Jesus Christ is our Lord, that is, our Master. As slaves to Christ our focus must not be on wealth and prosperity, but rather, on doing our master's business. The New Testament demands that the Church submits to Christ, just as the slave submitted to his master. The gospel was not given to facilitate personal ambition and gratification. Jesus is not here to fulfill all our wishes. Rather, we, being His slaves, are here to fulfill His wishes. Christ is the Master of all true Christians. True Christians have given over their lives to Him. Christ owns the believer. We are His possession. We are His slaves. Christ, unlike the human slave master, is a master that calls us friends and treats us with agape love. Christ's yoke is easy, and His burden is light. (Matthew 11:30, KJV).

This is the position, and what is expected, of the servant. But what is expected of the master? In the past, scriptures like these found in Luke 17:7-10, have been used by oppressors to justify slavery and other forms of injustices while most of the 'institutionalized church' maintained an uncomfortable silence. My use of the term 'institutionalized church' here is somewhat of an oxymoron. The Church does not exist as an institution but rather, as a body of people (believers). A church that condones an injustice and never raises a cry against injustice may very well be a church that endorses injustice. To truly desire to see the Church brought back to its rightful position in Christ, we will have to be true to ourselves, and examine, and repent of some grievous sins of our fathers.

Many have, for selfish reasons, operated their nefarious activities using Christianity as a justification for their actions. Mine is not to excuse the Church for its moral failures in the past or even in the present. The Church must take responsibility for its malfeasance or nonfeasance and repent accordingly. If need be, it should also make restitution. This is not only the way of Christ; it is the way to Christ. The subject of slavery is a very touchy one. While there is no verse in the New Testament that expressly forbids or condemns slavery, Jesus preached a message of love and told the parable of the good Samaritan to show man the injustices that his heart should not condone. History shows that the Church did not play the most prominent of roles in the abolition of slavery. The Church of Jesus Christ had been hijacked by white slave masters who sought to use religion to perpetuate their self-interests in the slave trade. The Church of the 16th to 19th century, influenced by white slave owners, bastardized - and manipulated - the Christian faith. They emphasized that the slave had a pious obligation of absolute submission to his slave master. They concluded that the principle that all men were equal in Christ did not mean that they were socially and economically equal. The churches of the 16th to 19th centuries were not known to condemn slavery as an institution. Some of the churches preached kindness to slaves but hardly condemned slavery. This was not surprising as many of the churches owned slaves and so were interested in maintaining the status quo.

George Whitefield, a prominent Anglican Episcopal preacher in the 18th century, upheld slavery. Often, justification for the most inhumane treatment of man was found in the Bible - the same Bible that has repentance and redemption as its central theme. Indeed, the human heart is deceitful and desperately wicked. Some prominent preachers of the 18th and 19th century were known to be brutal slave masters. These atrocities continued while churches for the most part were silent. The Methodist Church at its Annual General Conference in Georgia, circa 1836, held that slavery as it existed in the United States was not a moral evil. The Methodist Church renounced any insinuation that it had held slavery to be evil in the past (*An Appeal to the Methodist Episcopal Church by Orange Scott, 1838*). This attitude was not peculiar to the Methodist Church. The New York Presbyterian Church in 1836 resolved that no one should be elected into the office of deacon or elder unless they pledged not to discuss the matter of slavery. The protestant episcopal churches had declared, around this same period, that unless there was a new revelation from heaven, no one was authorized to judge slavery as evil. The Methodist Church in Cincinnati directly opposed the abolition of slavery and distanced itself from the abolitionists. It was difficult for many of these churches to denounce slavery because a substantial part of their funding came from slave owners. The churches acquiesced while powerful slave owners dominated the power structure of the churches and determined the direction the churches would go. The Church has a moral duty to repent and be cleansed from the scourge of this heinous sin. To truly represent Christ, the bride must become like her bridegroom.

In the United States, the 13th amendment abolished slavery in December 1865. While it would seem that the church would not have to contend with slavery issues anymore, there are still the aftershocks of slavery that pop up every now and then. Slavery gave birth to racial inequalities and prejudices that plague many parts of the world today, especially America. The Church has a leading role to play in resolving these recurring societal injustices.

The Church in the Era of Segregation

It must be acknowledged that in Christ, there is only one Church. However, divisions have often arisen within the Church of Christ as was the case in the Corinthian church. For the sake of clarity, we will address this man-made division by referring to 'white' churches and the 'black' churches. After the civil war in America, many white churches were known to actively support a racial hierarchy that placed the white population above other races. By extension, this meant that the institutionalized white church of that era also supported the view that the white believers were superior to other racial classes of believers. A substantial majority of the white churches endorsed the government policies that segregated the races. The church of this era accepted slavery as a part of life and a part of the economic system. There was even a conspiracy between many of the churches and those that benefited from slavery to keep the Bible away from the minority black population. For example, with the tacit approval of the mainstream church during the slave era, another Bible, with substantial editions and redactions was handed over to the black slaves. This adulterated Bible excluded the book of Exodus so that the black slaves would not be inspired to revolt for their liberty. That Bible excluded portions of Scripture that dealt with liberty and love, and included portions of Scripture that demanded slaves to obey their masters. The Museum of the Bible in Washington, D.C. is a good place to visit and understand these historical facts and to also understand the manipulative role the Church has played over the centuries.

The exclusive white church had justified slavery and later, segregation, by using the Bible for that purpose. Thomas Jefferson, the third President of the United States, had stated that all men were created equal and yet he was responsible for enslaving so many of his fellow men. Such was the hypocrisy at the time and sections of the Church played along as a beneficiary. Then there was George Whitfield, a well-known evangelist and gospel preacher that argued for the legalization of slavery and viewed the black slaves as subordinate humans. It is important to note however that there were some Christians of the time that spoke and fought against the injustices of slavery and segregation. The Quakers embarked on an anti-slavery campaign. The abolitionist movement in the North began to pick up steam and eventually, the institutionalized church consisting of only the white population now appeared to have a change of heart. But this change of heart was yet to be reflected in how the Church viewed non-whites.

Segregation in the United States was a systemic state policy backed by law. Segregation invariably meant that there was no genuine fellowship between white believers and the black believers. Segregation preached that only birds of the same feather must flock together. It betrays the New Testament principle that the Church is one body united in the love and

Spirit of Christ. The evil of segregation stunted fellowship and implied that the whites and the blacks were not united in Christ. Segregation conferred many benefits and privileges on the white church establishment and most of the white churches gladly accepted that. The Ku Klux Klan (KKK) was sometimes welcomed in some of these churches. Obviously, the mainstream church of the time did not preach against the injustices of the KKK. Rather, it took the efforts of civil rights activists like Martin Luther King to force a change. Victory over segregation, and to a minor extent, discrimination was spearheaded and driven by the black churches with a few white churches lending genuine support. Advocacy for civil rights grew out of the black church communities and was championed by the black church. Many white churches kept quiet when confronted with the injustices of segregation, and the police brutality against blacks, because it did not adversely affect them. In fact, it benefitted them. Similarly, many churches today keep quiet over same sex marriages and abortions. At these relevant times in history, can it truly be said that the Church had not drifted from Christ? Bringing the Church back to Christ is indeed an onerous task that can only be accomplished by God's grace. The bride must make herself ready (Revelation 19:7) to be joined with Christ.

In the era of segregation, it was unheard of that a black preacher would preach in a white church. Yet, the Church kept engaging in hypocrisy by preaching the love of God and the love of neighbor. God commands His people to love their neighbors as Christ loved them. When love was preached, the litmus test became can that neighbor of yours with a different color skin marry your daughter? Often the attitude displayed was that: "I love my neighbor of color, but I do not want him to move into my neighborhood." It is recorded that in 1959, less than 0.03 percent of the 100,000 white churches in the South could boast of a black member (*Equal Justice Initiative, January 1, 2016*). Till today in America, the Church of Christ is yet to heal and fully integrate. The wounds of the past run deep. There have been claims of mutual forgiveness, but the fruit of forgiveness, healing, and restoration are yet to mature. Mutual suspicion, lack of trust, and the playing of politics appear to be more prevalent in integrated churches. The way America is going, we are bound to see less diverse churches as the socio-economic gap between the races is widened. Some blacks are comfortable in their black churches. They see the black church as a place of refuge on Sundays. The black church gives them some relief from the elements of racism that they may have experienced all week. On the other hand, some whites in the integrated churches have spoken of having to walk on eggshells so as not to offend non-whites, especially, blacks. Pastors with racially diverse congregations will have to do more work to ensure that there is racial harmony in their churches. For the church in America to truly become racially inclusive, there must be repentance of the sins of the fathers and a genuine embracing of the love of Christ.

> A new commandment I give unto you, that ye love one another, as I have loved you, that ye also love one another. (John 13:34, KJV).

The Church and the Holocaust

From about 1938, the Jews were discriminated and persecuted by the Italian fascist regime that consisted of many professing to be Christians. In the course of World War II – (1938 – 1945) - Nazi Germany had exterminated over 10 million Jews in the Holocaust. Many Jews were taken to concentration camps and killed enmasse. The anti-Semitism propaganda of the Nazis and Fascists found support in the European "Christian" environment that had harbored anti-Semitism for decades. This group of so-called Christians, with such hatred for Jews, created a platform for the Nazis to justify their own rather intense variation of anti-Semitism. In a sense, the Holocaust was committed by persons professing to be Christians in the epicenter of Christendom. Men like Martin Luther did not help matters with his anti-Semitic writings of centuries prior. Martin Luther spearheaded the breaking away of the Protestant Church from the Catholic Church. Yet, Martin Luther is credited as saying, in his writings, that the Jews "daily blaspheme and slander our Lord Jesus Christ. Since they do this and we know about it, we should not tolerate it. For if I tolerate in my midst someone who slanders, blasphemes, and curses my Lord Jesus Christ, then I make myself a participant in the sins of another." Martin Luther went as far as calling for the Jews to be driven away and not to be regarded as brothers. This kind of attitude stoked the fires of anti-Semitism that reared its ugly head in Nazi Germany from 1939 – 1945. Adolf Hitler and many of his officers were professing Catholics or Christians and yet the Catholic Church did not deem it necessary to excommunicate them. While Hitler executed his Final Solution against the Jews, none of the churches opposed it publicly. The loud silence and complacency of the church with respect to anti-Semitism during the Holocaust has festered recurring wounds in the relationship between Christianity and Judaism. It will take a concerted effort on the part of both parties to build trust. Of recent, the church has taken an interest in supporting Israel financially and in other ways. Nonetheless, the purported neutrality of the institutionalized church in Europe during the Holocaust contradicted the teachings of Jesus Christ.

In the parable of the good Samaritan recorded in Luke 10:25-37, a traveler was robbed on his journey, stripped of his clothing, injured, and left half-dead. A priest saw him and passed by on the other side. Likewise, a Levite looked at him and passed by on the other side. However, a Samaritan saw him and took compassion on him. The Samaritan went to him and bandaged his wounds, pouring on oil and wine; and he set the man that was left half-dead on his own animal, brought him to an inn, and took care of him. The Samaritan gave the inn keeper some money to take care of the injured man. Jesus told this parable to show that the person that showed the love of a neighbor was not necessarily the one with a title but rather, the one that went out of his way and made a sacrifice by seeing to the restoration of his fellowman. The true Church must demonstrate the love of Christ to the least of these whenever she is in a position to do so. The voice of the Church must be heard in the face of victimization, oppression, and injustice.

The Role of the Church in Apartheid South Africa

Just like in the Holocaust, some of the prominent churches in South Africa played an instrumental role in legitimizing apartheid as a state policy in South Africa. Apartheid facilitated and enforced racial discrimination and segregation in South Africa. It created a racial hierarchy where the white minority population was at the apex and the black majority population were at the bottom. The Dutch Reformed Church of South Africa provided all sorts of convoluted biblical justifications for apartheid. This church claimed that by God scattering the people and giving them different languages at the tower of Babel, God wanted them to be separated. And so the white congregations of South Africa excluded black worshipers from being a part of their fellowship. Worse still, many in white South Africa did not acknowledge blacks as human beings. It came to a point when the black South African was disenfranchised in his own land. In 1953, the white government passed the Bantu Education Act whose purpose was to ensure that the black African always received a subservient education. Most churches in South Africa opposed the Act with the exception of the Lutheran Church and the Dutch Reformed Church.

With apartheid came restrictions on freedom of worship and association. Apartheid created a deliberate racial prejudice among the population. Racial prejudice is a pre-determined judgment against people of a different skin color. Pseudo-Christian justifications were often given to validate these evil practices and the laws that backed them up. For instance, a church with white members but a black majority was restricted from acquiring property in white areas. Thus, the rights of Africans to worship at a place of their choice was restricted. In somewhat similar fashion, the rights of whites and colored people were also restricted by the requirement that they obtained special permits to visit black churches. Why were many powerful white churches reluctant to advocate for change? The simple reason was that many of their members had a stake in maintaining a skewed status quo that favored themselves. Implementing the gospel's cry for righteousness and justice was far from their thinking as far as it related to other races. Again and again, the Church's complacency, and purported neutrality in the face of great injustices has often led to the conclusion that the Church did not exist to lift up man but rather to preserve her own parochial interests.

From Pentecost until now, true to the word of Christ in Matthew 16:18, nothing thrown at the Church has prevailed against her. Besides persecution, the church has been placed in positions where she sought to adapt in order to survive. Christ had emphasized to the earlier disciples that even though the Church is in the world, the Church is not of the world. Often times, in an attempt to adapt to her environment, the Church has compromised on her core values of love and being a light in the darkness. The Church, if viewed as a human institution, has kept quiet at critical times when she ought to have been outspoken. At other times, in order to be politically correct, the Church has been loosely connected to Christ in a futile attempt to serve two masters. In order to return to her rightful position in Christ, the Church must be willing to fall to the ground like that kernel of wheat and die in order to grow in her relevance and fruitfulness. Falling to the ground like that kernel of wheat will require a thorough and radical self-examination that will lead to a genuine repentance of the sinful attitudes and acts of the past. Indeed, many aspects of the history of the institutionalized church can be likened to the fathers eating sour grapes that have caused the teeth of the children to be set on edge. (Ezekiel 18:2). It is important that members of the body of Christ become conversant with these matters so that they know how to pray and intercede for reconciliation.

CHAPTER THREE

THE SEVEN CHURCHES IN REVELATION

"God doesn't give the hardest battles to His toughest soldiers.
He creates the toughest soldiers through life's hardest battles."
Unknown Author

Overview of the Book of Revelation

The book of Revelation records and outlines the revelation of the person and the prophetic program of Jesus Christ. It reveals prophetic events that will occur on earth prior to and at the second coming of Jesus Christ. Jesus Christ shared this revelation with the apostle John so that the Church will be encouraged to persevere through the persecution, sufferings, and hardships that was upon them and that was still to come. The book of Revelation establishes the victory that Christ won for the believer at the Cross of Calvary. The victory of Christ over the world and Satan is illustrated in Revelation. Christ shall judge and put an end to all unrighteousness. The plan of God as evidenced in the book of Revelation is that the saints will reign with Christ and must be willing to endure to the very end. On the other hand, Satan, the beast, the false prophet, those that worshipped the beast, and all unbelievers will be cast into the lake of fire for all eternity. At the time that the apostle John wrote the book of Revelation, many of the churches had backslidden in their relationship with Christ due to persecution and the rise of teachers of heresy. Some believers had lost hope in the second coming of Christ and in the resurrection. The book of Revelation displays and exemplifies the supremacy of Jesus Christ. The early chapters of Revelation were written to encourage the churches in Asia Minor to remain in Christ even in the midst of severe persecution.

Revelation highlights the ancient struggle that exists between forces of good and forces of evil. It presents the conflict between those that have faith in Christ and those that do not. Eventually God will intervene in the conflict by handing over the right to judge His enemies to Jesus Christ. This is seen when Christ - the Lamb of God, takes the scroll of judgment with seven seals from the hand of God the Father. (Revelation 5:6-7). The judgments that are in the book of Revelation emanate from this scroll and start occurring rapidly, and perhaps sometimes simultaneously, as Christ opens the seven seals, followed by the sounding of the seven trumpets, and the pouring out of the contents of the seven bowls. When the seventh angel sounds his trumpet, then will we see the kingdom of the world become the kingdom of the Lord Jesus Christ, and He will reign for ever and ever (Revelation 11:15). The book of Revelation is 'not necessarily' best understood by viewing it in a strict chronological order. Rather, a better approach may be to view it as a revelation of what must soon take place (Revelation 1:1). Nonetheless, the book of Revelation can be seen as covering a historical period and a period that remains in the future. The historical period which still speaks in the present day is covered in the first three chapters of Revelation. The first three chapters deal with the introduction of Jesus Christ as the One furnishing the Revelation followed by His message to the seven churches. In Chapter Four of Revelation, heaven was opened unto John and Jesus invited the apostle John to "Come up here, and I will show you *what must take place after this.*" (Revelation 4:1, NIV). (Emphasis in italics is mine.) Revelation 4:1 transitions the Revelation of Jesus Christ from what had been previously revealed to the apostle John to 'what must take place after this'. The latter relates to the future. Revelation 1:19 divides the book of Revelation into three parts: what John saw, what is now and what will take place later.

> Write the things which thou hast seen, and the things which are, and the things which shall be hereafter. (Revelation 1:19, KJV).

In Revelation 1:19, KJV, *"the things which thou hast seen"*, the things which John saw at this point related to his encounter with Jesus Christ in Revelation 1. *"The things which are"* relate to John's current state of affairs where he has to write down and deliver the messages to the seven churches. The things which shall be hereafter relate to the events occurring from Revelation 4:1.

The book of Revelation gives us a glimpse of activities occurring at the throne of God in heaven. We see elders, living creatures and thousands upon thousands of angels worshipping God Almighty. In the course of the judgments during the Great Tribulation, God sends His two witnesses that were given power to shut down heaven, to turn waters into blood, and to smite the earth with all manner of plagues. In Revelation 13, we see devil worshipping being instituted on the earth and men taking the mark of the beast. In Revelation 17 and 18, we see Mystery Babylon being judged and rendered desolate. In Revelation 19, we are shown the marriage supper of the Lamb. Revelation 19 records the capture of the beast, the false prophet, and their entourage. Following their capture, they were cast alive into the lake of fire burning with brimstone. Revelation 20 covers the millennial reign of Christ, the release of Satan from the bottomless pit for a season pending his being cast also into the lake of fire. Also in Revelation 20, the apostle John saw a great white throne where God sat to deliver judgment. The books were opened. Another book was opened which is 'the book of life'. (Revelation 20:12, KJV). The dead were judged according to their works. Death and hell were cast into the lake of fire. This is the second death. Anyone whose name was not found written in the book of life was thrown into the lake of fire. Many churches these days rarely preach about heaven and hell. Many believers are oblivious to the fact that heaven and hell are real. In bringing the Church back to Christ, those the Lord called into the pulpit ministry must not fail to warn the people that the wages of sin is death and that the gift of God is eternal life in Christ Jesus. The soul that sinneth shall die. Many churches are preaching a user-friendly, watered-down type of gospel. In doing so, they have drifted away from Christ. The Church must brace up and warn her congregants of the danger of going to hell fire for all of eternity. We must repent of preaching that bogus gospel that says, "once saved, always saved."

We are in the era where many believers do not fear God. The teaching that salvation without living righteously is sufficient before God is a teaching not found in the Bible. While we are not saved by good works, we are saved to do good works. Many have come before church altars and said the sinner's prayer without genuine repentance. The fruit of their lives have shown that they are not that new creation in Christ that the New Testament talks about. In salvation, there must be genuine repentance and faith working together. An abuse of grace has been encouraged by a false lackadaisical teaching that emphasizes that you can live life as you please and still get to be in heaven. The truth is that the grace of Christ demands repentance and holiness. Every other grace is cheap and merely provides a license to sin. A gospel that encourages sin and that abuses the grace of Christ is not a gospel that is of Christ. Many churches would have to re-examine their teachings on Salvation to ensure that they are not outside of Christ.

Revelation 21 presents the new heaven and the new earth with a new Jerusalem. Jesus gives a promise: He that overcometh shall inherit all things; and I will be his God, and he shall be my son. (Revelation 21:7). However, the fearful, and unbelieving, and the abominable, and murderers, and whoremongers, and sorcerers, and idolaters, and all liars, shall have their part in the lake which burneth with fire and brimstone: which is the second death. (Revelation 21:8). We must diligently and dutifully warn the world, and the churches that there is a second death which ushers the souls of men, for all of eternity, into the lake which burneth with fire and brimstone. Those that will be cast into the lake of fire and brimstone for all eternity include the fearful, the unbelieving, and all liars.

In the final chapter of the book of Revelation (Chapter 22), we are shown the return of the tree of life which man was forbidden to approach in the garden of Eden after the fall of man. When Christ has put an end to all rebellion and sin, there shall be no more curse. Blessed are they that do His commandments, that they may have right to the tree of life, and may enter in through the gates into the city. (Revelation 22:14). As believers, we must be trained to follow God's commandments so that we may partake of the tree of life and enter in through the gates into the city of God.

The Rapture

The Rapture is an event that will cause the dead in Christ and we that are alive in Christ to be caught up to meet with Christ in the air. The Bible provides us with some glimpses of what to expect at the Rapture. We see a type of this with Enoch in Genesis 5:24: Enoch walked with God; then he was no more, because God took him away. The book of Second Kings records in Chapter 2 how Elijah went up to heaven in a whirlwind, as soon as a chariot of fire and horses of fire appeared and separated him from Elisha. This also gives us a hint of the Rapture that is destined to occur any time from now. The Rapture will cause the true Church of Christ - the true believers - to be separated from those that do not know Christ. At the Rapture, the true Church will be taken up to meet with Christ and the false church shall be left behind. Again, in Acts 1:9, we see this spiritual phenomenon of the Rapture being revealed.

> And when he had spoken these things, while they beheld, he was taken up; and a cloud received him out of their sight. And while they looked steadfastly toward heaven as he went up, behold two men stood by them in white apparel; which also said, Ye men of Galilee, why stand ye gazing up into heaven? *This same Jesus which is taken up from you into heaven,* shall so come in like manner as ye have seen him go into heaven. (Acts 1:9-11, KJV). (Emphasis in italics is mine.)

The Bible speaks in clear terms of the Rapture of the Church in 1 Thessalonians 4:13-18, KJV:

> [13] But I would not have you to be ignorant, brethren, concerning them which are asleep, that ye sorrow not, even as others which have no hope. [14] For if we believe that Jesus died and rose again, even so them also which sleep in Jesus will God bring with him. [15] For this we say unto you by the word of the Lord, that we which are alive and remain unto the coming of the Lord shall not prevent them which are asleep. [16] For the Lord himself shall descend from heaven with a shout, with the voice of the archangel, and with the trump of God: and the dead in Christ shall rise first: [17] Then we which are alive and remain shall be caught up together with them in the clouds, to meet the Lord in the air: and so shall we ever be with the Lord. [18] Wherefore comfort one another with these words.

Various schools of thought exist relating to when the Rapture will occur in the prophetic timeline of the Great Tribulation. I am firmly of the conviction that the true church, which is the bride of Christ, will be taken away, (raptured), prior to the events that Jesus was about to show the apostle John in Revelation 4. It can be inferred from the Word of God, that the Rapture would mark the end of the church age on earth. The judgments and victories of Christ at the Great Tribulation shall usher in the reign of the Kingdom of God on earth. The next significant event in the revealed prophetic timeline of God is the Rapture. The Church is raptured prior to the Great Tribulation. In Revelation 3:10, Jesus tells the church at Philadelphia that since they had kept His command to endure patiently, he will also keep them from the hour of trial that is coming on the whole world to test those who live on the earth. This is referring to the Great Tribulation. God did not appoint the believer to suffer His wrath but rather, to receive salvation through the Lord Jesus Christ. (1 Thessalonians 5:9, KJV).

It is instructive to note that after the apostle John presents the messages to the seven churches, the Church does not appear again in the book of Revelation until the 19th Chapter at the marriage supper of the Lamb. This lends credence to the viewpoint that the Church is raptured prior to the events of the Great Tribulation.

Revelation Chapter 1

Christ's message to the seven churches in Asia Minor is found in Chapters Two and Three of Revelation. Before we examine Christ's messages to the churches, it helps to get a good understanding of where Christ is coming from and how He is communicating His message. Revelation 1 affords us that opportunity.

> ¹The Revelation of Jesus Christ, which God gave unto him, to shew unto his servants things which must shortly come to pass; and he sent and signified it by his angel unto his servant John: ²Who bare record of the word of God, and of the testimony of Jesus Christ, and of all things that he saw. ³Blessed is he that readeth, and they that hear the words of this prophecy, and keep those things which are written therein: for the time is at hand. (Revelation 1:1-3, KJV).

In Revelation 1:1, it is clear that the revelation that is being presented here is that of Jesus Christ and not of the apostle John. A chain of communication is evident here: the revelation came from God the Father to Jesus Christ to an angel and then to John. In other words, God the Father gave the Revelation to Jesus Christ. Jesus Christ in turn gave it to an angel. The angel gave it to the apostle John. The angel did not have much to do with the message other than to deliver it. The message had nothing to do with the angel that was employed in its delivery. The revelation concerned "things which must shortly come to pass." In Revelation 1:1, "Things which must shortly come to pass," means that once the day for fulfillment comes, there will be no delay in its execution. Christ wanted the apostle John to tell the churches these things. In Revelation 1:2, John bares record of the word of God. In other words, John was merely a witness of what he saw by revelation and made a written record of it.

> Behold, he cometh with clouds; and every eye shall see him, and they also which pierced him: and all kindreds of the earth shall wail because of him. Even so, Amen. (Revelation 1:7, KJV).

Revelation 1:7 gives us the theme of the Book of Revelation which is the second coming of Christ. Thus, the churches ought to be preparing for His return.

In Revelation 1:10-11, KJV, John was in the Spirit. He heard a loud voice behind him like a trumpet, which said: "I am Alpha and Omega, the first and the last: and, What thou seest, write in a book, and send it unto the seven churches which are in Asia; unto Ephesus, and unto Smyrna, and unto Pergamos, and unto Thyatira, and unto Sardis, and unto Philadelphia, and unto Laodecia." When John turned around to see the voice that was speaking to him, he saw seven golden lampstands and among the lampstands, someone like unto the Son of man. His head and hair were white as wool, as white as snow, and His eyes were like a blazing fire. His voice was like the sound of rushing waters and in His right hand were seven stars. Out of His mouth came a sharp double-edged sword. His face was like the sun shining in all its brilliance. When apostle John saw the resurrected Christ, he fell at His feet as though dead. The Church today needs this vision of Christ. The Church needs to get to a place where we fall at His feet as though dead. In Revelation 1:17-18, Jesus then introduces

Himself to John as the first and the last. "I am he that liveth, and was dead; and behold, I am alive forevermore, Amen; and have the keys of hell and of death". (Revelation 1:18). Jesus then instructs John to write what he has seen, what is now and what will take place later. He tells John the mystery of the seven golden lampstands and seven stars in His right hand. The seven stars are the angels of the seven churches, and the seven lampstands are the seven churches.

Our local churches today have lessons to learn from the message of Christ that apostle John delivered to the seven churches. Many of our local churches need to be set in order. In these end times, the Lord is issuing a clarion call for His people to put their houses in order. The letters to the seven churches will help us see things from the viewpoint of Jesus Christ and hopefully, encourage us to make the necessary adjustments.

The Message to the Church at Ephesus

Christ introduces Himself to the church at Ephesus as the One who holds the seven stars in His right hand and walks among the seven golden lampstands. He then informs this church that He has divine knowledge of their works, their labor, and their patience. In fact, Jesus tells all seven churches that He knows their works.

> [2] I know thy works, and thy labor, and thy patience, and how thou canst not bear them which are evil: and thou hast tried them which say they are apostles, and are not, and hast found them liars: [3] And hast borne, and hast patience, and for my name's sake hast labored, and hast not fainted. (Revelation 2:2-3, KJV).

Jesus also lets the church at Ephesus know that He knows that they cannot tolerate wicked men, and that they have tested those who claim to be apostles and have found them to be false. So this is a church that has good works. In addition, Christ commends them for persevering and enduring hardship for His name's sake and for not growing weary. The church at Ephesus had good works but, faith and love were missing. The Ephesian church trying the so-called apostles and finding them to be liars shows that this was a church that had sound doctrine. They knew the truth of the

Gospel. For the sake of Christ, the church at Ephesus labored and fainted not. In other words, they took a stand for righteousness regardless of the price. In spite of the challenges and hardships they faced, they persevered and did not quit. This church abounded in the work of the Lord.

In seeking to bring the modern day, end time Church back to Christ, what lessons can be learned from the church at Ephesus?

The first thing today's churches must understand is that Christ knows their works, whether good or bad. Nothing is hidden from Him. His eyes are a flaming fire that can examine the heart of man. All are naked before Him. Christ will weigh every motive, and every intent behind our actions and thoughts. And so it is important that the Church of God understands that there is a day of reckoning.

Unlike the church in Ephesus that could not bear them which were evil, a significant number of our modern-day churches are unequally yoked with them that are evil. Some churches go as far as hiring worldly musicians to lead their praise and worship during their Sunday services and other gatherings. I recall visiting a church in Brooklyn, New York that employed worldly musicians to play their instruments for them during their church meetings. As soon as the musicians finished playing, and while the church service was still going on, they went outside to smoke and jest. Worldly musicians of questionable character are being put on church stages to perform the Lord's songs. To the Lord, this might as well be, not the offering of a sacrifice of praise but rather, a strange fire. From what we can see of the church at Ephesus, they would not have stood for such nonsense. They could not bear them which were evil. Many of today's churches have allowed the influence of the world into the Lord's sanctuaries in order to advance their status in society. They have partnered with the ungodly all in an attempt to enhance their social status. They have courted the services of wicked men in order to grow their congregations. For instance, some pastors do not mind compromising the gospel message if that will give them time on television. Some had been told not to mention the name of Jesus or the blood of Jesus during a television broadcast and they gladly agreed to this. They have yielded to the demands of the ungodly, all for the sake of a mess of porridge. The church in Ephesus was a church that stood its ground when it came to contending for the gospel.

A second thing today's churches can learn from the church at Ephesus is that they were a church that tested the spirits. They tested those that claimed to be apostles of Christ and found them to be liars. How many

Christians today can recognize a false apostle? Many cannot because they too are false Christians. Today, so many false pastors, prophets, apostles, and ministers, parade themselves in church pulpits. They are wolves in sheep clothing. This could not happen in Ephesus because the church there would have tested them to see what material they were made of. When we allow false ministers into our churches, it destroys the credibility of our testimony in Christ. Many churches go from one scandal to another, be it financial, sexual, or political all because the spirits within are not tested. Seducing spirits have taken over many churches with false men of God performing false signs and wonders. Unfortunately, these churches glory in signs and wonders without testing to see the source of power from which the signs and wonders flow.

The Ephesian church had borne with patience for the sake of Christ's name and labored without fainting. To bear with patience means that they had endured hardship for a considerable period without complaining and without growing weary. Christ commended the Ephesian church for demonstrating this character. How many true believers today can endure a rough trial without complaining and without quitting? Christ expects us to be able to bear hardship without complaining and growing weary. In 2 Timothy 2:3, we are admonished to endure hardness as good soldiers of Jesus Christ.

> Nevertheless I have somewhat against thee because thou hast left thy first love. Remember therefore from whence thou art fallen, and repent, and do the first works; or else I will come unto thee quickly, and remove thy candlestick out of its place, except thou repent. (Revelation 2:4-5, KJV).

In Revelation 2:4, Christ is grieved because this church, in spite of her good works, had forsaken her first love (Christ). They had not lost their first love. They had forsaken Him. They had neglected Christ while doing the work of Christ. The original spiritual vitality of the church had been replaced by a routine of orthodoxy. They demonstrated zeal without showing love for Christ. They had fallen and needed to repent quickly. Likewise, so many churches today are engaged in lots of programs and activities and may not necessarily have a healthy relationship with their first love, Jesus Christ. Such churches may be quick to debate doctrinal positions and to show that they are right and that others are wrong. However, when love is lacking, it all becomes meaningless. A church that does not have love amounts to nothing. (1 Corinthians 13:2).

The challenge for the Church in these end times is to maintain her first love. We must not follow the example of the church at Ephesus that did good works by total reliance on their own strength and abilities. Maintaining our first love demands that the church depends solely on Christ: "If any man will come after me, let him deny himself, and take up his Cross daily, and follow me." (Luke 9:23, KJV).

In Revelation 2:5, the only thing that could redeem the church at Ephesus was their repenting. Their failure to do so would risk their candlestick being removed from its place. This means that failure to repent can cause the church to lose her candlestick, that is, her ability to give light. Many churches are no longer emitting the light of the gospel in a world filled with darkness. Many churches need to repent as Christ may have removed their candlestick from its place. They are calling on the name of Jesus, but the presence of God is no longer with them. When they meet, the presence of God is not evident. Their meetings and fellowship are so dry and stale. They need to repent in order to restore broken fellowship with God. Repentance will bring back the presence of God into these churches.

However, the church at Ephesus still gets commended for hating the deeds of the Nicolaitans which Christ also hated. (Revelation 2:6). The Nicolaitans exerted rigid control over the lay congregation. *Nico* in Greek means control. *Laitans* means laity.

The church in Ephesus is instructed by Christ to repent and do their first works. To do the first works means that the church must go back to the place they were before they deviated. That place is at the Cross of Christ where salvation was made possible.

The Message to the Church at Smyrna

> I know thy works, and tribulation, and poverty, (but thou art rich) and I know the blasphemy of them which say they are Jews, and are not, but are the synagogue of Satan. Fear none of those things which thou shall suffer: behold, the devil shall cast some of you into prison, that ye may be tried; and ye shall have tribulation ten days: be thou

faithful unto death, and I will give thee a crown of life. (Revelation 2:9-10, KJV).

The believers in the church of Smyrna had been experiencing grave persecution. As a result, they had been reduced to poverty. Unbelieving Jews blasphemed against their faith and reviled against them. The church at Smyrna is not reprimanded by Jesus Christ but is admonished to endure suffering and tribulation faithfully. Jesus tells this church that by their faithful perseverance even unto death, He will bestow upon them the crown of life. In Revelation 2:11, Jesus promises the church in Smyrna that for their overcoming they will not be hurt by the second death.

Many modern-day churches have drifted from the Spirit of Christ and need to draw nearer to Christ. There are a few lessons we can take from Jesus' message to the church at Smyrna.

First and foremost, in spite of being reduced to poverty by ongoing persecution, Christ stated that this church was rich. Christ does not measure richness in terms of dollars and cents, in terms of gold and silver, and not in terms of other earthly possessions. Those churches that thirst after money should learn from this narrative that money is not the measure of true riches in the sight of God. A church can be financially wealthy and yet, spiritually bankrupt.

Jesus told the church at Smyrna not to fear the things which they were bound to suffer. A believer that is fearful of what he will have to suffer for the sake of Christ would more easily compromise his faith in order to escape suffering. Many times, as we saw in the previous chapter of this book, the Church had maintained a silence in order not to go through suffering. Jesus tells this church to be faithful unto death. How many of us Christians that constitute the Church can be faithful even unto death? Jesus is letting the end time Church know that sometimes the gospel will require us to pay the ultimate price by laying down our lives. When tested, as Christians, we must show ourselves faithful even to the point of death, as opposed to convenience. Are you only faithful when it is convenient? Can you be faithful even to the point of death? Your life is characterized by your faithfulness. Similarly, the life of the Church is characterized by its faithfulness.

When persecution comes to the Church, as bad as it is, it will have the effect of clearing away the hypocrites and the uncommitted out of the Church. Persecution has a way of separating the wheat from the chaff and strengthening the faith of the Church. In a church where there is more chaff than wheat, the church will readily compromise to avoid persecution. However, the church at Smyrna was not like that. They were willing to endure persecution even unto death. Churches in times of ease and prosperity are quick to confess Christ as Lord. Christ also expects that in perilous times, churches will do the same.

The Message to the Church at Pergamos

> [13] I know thy works, and where thou dwellest, even where Satan's seat is: and thou holdest fast my name, and hast not denied my faith, even in those days wherein Antipas was my faithful martyr, who was slain among you, where Satan dwelleth. [14] But I have a few things against thee, because thou hast there them that hold the doctrine of Balaam, who taught Balak to cast a stumblingblock before the children of Israel, to eat things sacrificed unto idols, and to commit fornication. [15] So hast thou also them that hold the doctrine of the Nicolaitans, which thing I hate. [16] Repent; or else I will come unto thee quickly, and will fight against them with the sword of my mouth. (Revelation 2:13-16, KJV).

The church in Pergamos dwelt where Satan's throne was. Nonetheless, some held fast to the faith and did not deny the name of Christ. Christ commended one of the faithful members of the church at Pergamos by the name, Antipas. Antipas was a faithful martyr of Christ that was slain among the brethren where Satan had his dwelling place. Some biblical scholars have claimed that the reference to the church dwelling where Satan had his seat meant that Satan had joined the church. Satan dwelt in this church through false doctrine such as the doctrine of the Nicolaitans. The church at Pergamos enjoyed worldly support. When a church is so loved and accepted by the world, it becomes doubtful whether Christ is at its center. It is a shameful thing to see many of our present-day churches seeking the attention, approval, and friendship of the world. Whenever the world is welcomed into the church, Satan also is welcomed. For our churches to be taken seriously, we spiritually must strive to cast out the spirit of worldliness that has so permeated the church.

Jesus mentioned a few things he had against the church in Pergamos. In returning to Christ, our churches today can learn from the sinful errors made at Pergamos. The doctrine of Balaam was prevalent in this church. Balaam was an Old Testament prophet hired by king Balak of Moab to ensnare Israel. Balaam yielded to king Balak's overtures and set a snare for Israel by prompting Israel's men to commit fornication with Moabite women. Balaam betrayed the God of Israel for the money that Balak had to offer. In similar fashion, for the love of money, many in the church are committing fornication with the spirit of the world. They have even gone as far as bringing their lover, the spirit of worldliness, into the church. Balaam, because of his love of money, seduced Israel to commit fornication with Moab. In the same way, the love of money has seduced many in churches to commit adultery with the world. Friendship with the world is enmity toward God. You cannot serve two masters. Many in the modern-day churches are striving in vain to serve two masters: God, and Marmon. Jesus makes it clear that he hates the doctrine of Balaam. This doctrine manipulates God's people for filthy lucre. Many have stumbled in the church because of a prosperity gospel movement that has elevated prosperity above the need for holiness and righteousness.

Besides adhering to the doctrine of Balaam, the church at Pergamos also endorsed the teachings of the Nicolaitans which Christ hated and which the church at Ephesus also hated. For all these, Christ warns this church to repent or else He will come quickly to make war against them with the sword of His mouth. It may very well be that Christ is fighting against many local churches with the sword of His mouth for their refusal to repent.

The Message to the Church at Thyatira

In His message to the church in Thyatira, Christ begins by commending the church for her charity, service, faith, patience, and ever-increasing good works. Nonetheless, Christ had a few things against them.

> [20] Notwithstanding I have a few things against thee, because thou sufferest that woman Jezebel, which calleth herself a prophetess, to teach and to seduce my servants to commit fornication, and to eat things sacrificed unto idols.

²¹ And I gave her space to repent of her fornication; and she repented not. ²² Behold, I will cast her into a bed, and them that commit adultery with her into great tribulation, except they repent of their deeds. ²³ And I will kill her children with death; and all the churches shall know that I am he which searcheth the reins and hearts: and I will give unto every one of you according to your works. ²⁴ But unto you I say, and unto the rest in Thyatira, as many as have not this doctrine, and which have not known the depths of Satan, as they speak; I will put upon you none other burden. ²⁵ But that which ye have already hold fast till I come. (Revelation 2: 20-25, KJV).

The main issue in the Thyatira church had to do with the presence and the role of Jezebel. Some biblical scholars have said that this Jezebel was an actual woman that existed in the church at Thyatira. Other scholars have maintained that there was no woman in the Thyatira church by the name of Jezebel, but that Christ uses the idolatress Jezebel of the Old Testament as a sort of allegory pointing towards spiritual adultery. One thing however is certain: the Jezebel anointing led to spiritual fornication and idolatry. Jezebel had ample opportunity to repent of her fornication but refused. Thus the church at Thyatira continued with Jezebel in their midst. Christ was against the church because they tolerated the corrupting presence and influence of Jezebel. If they failed to repent Christ promised to cast her into a bed of affliction, and to cast her adulterous partners into great tribulation. The church in Thyatira had allowed a false prophetess to teach and to seduce the servants of God. Some of the members of this church had not embraced Jezebel's teaching and had not learned Satan's so-called deep secrets. Jesus promised not to impose any other burden upon them. The churches of today have witnessed a rise in the number of Jezebel spirits being given positions of authority in God's house. These churches, if they refuse to repent, may suffer the same fate reserved for an unrepentant Thyatira church.

Jezebel is a manipulative witchcraft spirit that seeks to usurp God-appointed authority in the church. The spirit eventually disrupts order in the church and clandestinely begins to drive a satanic agenda that will quench the church's fire. The spirit of Jezebel targets church leadership, particularly prophetic church leadership. In this church in Thyatira,

Jezebel had assumed leadership by asserting herself in two out of the five-fold ministries: prophet, and teacher. Christ will never tolerate a spirit of witchcraft operating and leading in His house. And that is just what that Jezebel is. Subservient pastors with an Ahab spirit have sold their churches to strange powers. Where the pastor, as the angel of the church, and the Christ appointed authority in the church is no longer leading, then that church is in trouble. A pastor that merely preaches without providing leadership, guidance, and direction to the body of Christ has opened the door for usurping spirits to take over.

The Message to the Church at Sardis

> And to the angel of the church in Sardis write, These things says he who has the seven Spirits of God and the seven stars: "I know your works, that you have a name that you are alive, but you are dead. Be watchful, and strengthen the things which remain, that are ready to die, for I have not found your works perfect before God. Remember therefore how you have received and heard; hold fast and repent. Therefore if you will not watch, I will come upon you as a thief, and you will not know what hour I will come upon you ..." (Revelation 3:1-3, NKJV).

The church at Sardis had a reputation of being alive, but in reality, was a dead church. Today, in the world, there are many dead churches. From a distance they appear to be alive but when examined closely, it becomes apparent that they are dead. These types of churches make activities and programs the core of their mission and do not earnestly seek the anointing of the Holy Spirit. Jesus Christ must be the core of our mission. Christ must be the very center of the church or the church will end up operating as a dead church. The fire of the Holy Spirit provokes a lifestyle of revival. This was missing at Sardis. Christ had not found their works perfect before God. The works of the churches will be tested by Christ. Many churches are heavily invested in infrastructural edifices at the expense of souls. Their works will be tested. Many churches are heavily invested in social programs at the expense of the gospel. Their works also will be tested by Christ. For the works of the church to be found perfect before God, Jesus Christ must be the motive and the essence of the work. When a church spends millions of dollars in advertising itself rather than promoting the gospel of Jesus Christ, its work will be tested to see if it is perfect before God. Today the websites of some churches glorify the church or the pastor of the church. Christ will test these websites to see whether they truly represented Him or catered to the ego or agenda of an individual or group of individuals. When the works of some churches are tested in the fire, they may not endure because their material was made of wood and rubble.

The solution Christ prescribed for the church at Sardis was Repentance. It is the same solution that He is prescribing for many churches today that have drifted far away from Him. Christ does not reprimand the good with the bad in the church at Sardis. He recognizes those that had not defiled their garments. He promises that these ones shall walk with Him in white for they are worthy.

> He that overcometh, the same shall be clothed in white raiment; and I will not blot out his name out of the book of life, but I will confess his name before my Father, and before his angels. (Revelation 3:5, KJV).

Here, Jesus refers to blotting out names from the book of life. This therefore means that it is possible for a name to be blotted out of the book of life. This should cause many in the church to re-examine the doctrine of unconditional eternal security. The teaching that 'once saved, always saved' regardless of what the person does thereafter is not found in Scripture. It takes faith for one's name to be written in the book of life and if a person becomes apostate and unequivocally renounces his faith then such a person cannot be said to be a child of God. For the sake of clarity, God will not blot out a name from the book of life because of sin. If that were the case, there may be no names left in the book of life. Why did Christ talk of blotting out names from the book of life in Sardis? Why? Because they were dead! They had a reputation of being alive, but they were disconnected from the author of life. Those that have renounced the life of Christ in them are dead. The life of Christ is received by faith. Faith gets a person in the book of life and lack of faith gets him out.

Many churches have not properly taught the doctrine of Salvation. As a result, so many Christians are deceived into thinking that once they are "saved", they can do as they please. Faith without works is dead. A tree is known by its fruit. It is by your fruit that Christ determines your salvation. We are not saved by works but our works will either validate our faith or disprove it.

The Message to the Church at Philadelphia

> I know thy works: behold, I have set before thee an open door, and no man can shut it: for thou hast a little strength, and has kept my word, and hast not denied my name. (Revelation 3:8, KJV).

The church at Philadelphia was commended by Christ for her faithfulness in spite of her having only a little strength. In the world today, there are many churches that have grown in strength. Some of them are strong financially and strong numerically and yet, do not keep the Word of Christ. They may have merchandized and manipulated the Word of God to grow in strength. Strength in this sense is different from spiritual power. One may be physically strong, yet spiritually weak. The church at Philadelphia may have had little strength in terms of numbers but they demonstrated spiritual strength by keeping the Word of God and not denying the name of Christ. When there is mounting pressure as a result of lack of resources, many yield to the temptation to cut corners and compromise. This was not the case with the church at Philadelphia. Their little strength did not influence their faithfulness. Without underscoring the importance of finances, a spiritually strong church is one that keeps the Word of God and does not deny the name of Christ in her day to day existence. The church in Philadelphia stood their ground. They did not allow circumstances dictate what they would believe. To them, the Word of God was inerrant regardless of their experience. Today many local churches have revised the Word of God to reflect their rather limited experiences. Our experiences must be evaluated in the light of God's Word. We must not seek to validate God's Word by our own experiences. When a church does this, she reduces the Word of God, and by extension, reduces God to her level. God has magnified His Word above all His name. (Psalm 138:2). The church at Philadelphia understood this and remained true to the Word of God. The vitality of the spiritual life of a church is not solely measured by her strength and achievements, but rather by her obedience. The church in Philadelphia demonstrates that LITTLE is MUCH when God is in it. Churches that are small in number should not despise their size but learn to be faithful and content. Do not despise what is little. God created both the little and the big. Philadelphia was little and yet Christ let them know that He would make the so-called mighty of the synagogue of Satan to come and fall down at their feet and acknowledge that Christ had loved them. (Revelation 3:9). What matters is being faithful to Christ!

Keeping the word of Christ also means being subject to the right doctrine. Churches must always be at a place of humility where they are constantly subjecting themselves to self-examination. In 2 Corinthians 13:5, NIV, we are admonished: "Examine yourselves to see whether you are in the faith; test yourselves. Do you not realize that Christ Jesus is in you – unless, of course, you fail the test?" There is a strong likelihood that a considerable number of churches may fail this test simply because they may have grieved the Spirit of Christ or quenched the Spirit's fire. Churches should not just assume that Christ (the Word) is in them. The next and last of the seven churches we are about to look at briefly had Christ outside. Christ was knocking on the door to be let in.

The Message to the Church at Laodecia

> [15] I know thy works, that thou art neither cold nor hot: I would thou wert cold or hot. [16] So then because thou art lukewarm, and neither cold nor hot, I will spue thee out of my mouth. [17] Because thou sayest, I am rich, and increased with goods, and have need of nothing; and knowest not that thou art wretched, and miserable, and poor, and blind, and naked: [18] I counsel thee to buy of me gold tried in the fire, that thou mayest be rich; and white raiment, that thou mayest be clothed, and that the shame of thy nakedness do not appear; and anoint thine eyes with eyesalve, that thou mayest see. [19] As many as I love, I rebuke and chasten: be zealous therefore, and repent. [20] Behold, I stand at the door, and knock: if any man hear my voice, and open the door, I will come in to him, and will sup with him, and he with me. (Revelation 3:15-20, KJV).

The church in Laodecia is often referred to as the lukewarm church. Of the seven churches, the church in Laodecia is the only one that receives no commendation from Christ. Christ rebukes them for their complacency, self-sufficiency, and delusion. This church gloried in its earthly wealth and was deceived by it. Christ let them know that their true state was wretched, miserable, poor, blind, and naked. Their self-delusion resulted in their pitiable and miserable spiritual condition. To compound matters they were neither cold nor hot. This speaks of an apathy to the things in the heart of God. Many local churches have lost the fire of God in their midst. They are not hot. They have lost their zeal for the things of God such as prayer, evangelism, visiting the sick and those in prison, missions, and discipleship. They still engage in religious activities and so, are not cold. They are just lukewarm. They have a form of godliness in order to keep their doors open. Because they are lukewarm, they deny the power of God.

The church at Laodecia is a wayward congregation. Christ tells them that as many as He loves, He rebukes. Jesus' strong words of correction expresses His love for this church, and for this reason, He calls them to repent. In similar fashion, the voice of Christ can be heard in the land today inviting the erring churches to return to true fellowship with Him. The Church of God must repent and arise from spiritual lukewarmness and carry the burden to propagate the kingdom of God to the four corners of the earth.

CHAPTER FOUR

RETURNING TO THE CROSS OF CHRIST

"It was by his death that he wished above all else to be remembered. There is then, it is safe to say, no Christianity without the cross. If the cross is not central to our religion, ours is not the religion of Jesus."
John Stott, The Cross of Christ.

Prophecies of Christ's Crucifixion

The foundation of the Christian faith is predicated on the reality of Christ's death on the Cross and His resurrection three days afterwards. Jesus' death removed the barrier between sinful man and a sinless God. The obedience of Christ unto death on the Cross, in that His death was a sin offering, is the central theme of the gospel. Man's redemption was won on the Cross of Calvary. Without the finished work of Christ on the Cross, salvation of man would not have been accomplished. As we saw in Chapter Two of this book, Jesus Christ fulfilled all Old Testament prophecies given centuries before His birth. The Old Testament is replete with the mention and prescription of a sacrificial system to cover the sins of the people. This however was inadequate to atone for their sins. The Bible makes it clear in Hebrews 9:22 that without the shedding of blood there is no remission of sin. Hitherto, man had presented animal sacrifices to God to cover their sin. Jesus Christ came as the Lamb of God to take away the sins of the world. Even though Jesus is a King, He came as a lamb to be slaughtered on the Cross. Jesus is the only One that has and that could ever fulfill all the Old Testament prophecies relating to the Messiah. Jesus proved beyond the shadow of doubt that He is the Christ, the long-awaited Messiah. By being the only man born of a virgin, He fulfilled prophecy regarding how the Messiah would come and how he would be recognized. Jesus was born just to die. We shall briefly review a few of the Old Testament prophecies that relate to the Cross and the crucifixion of Jesus Christ. It is extremely important that our churches do not deviate or shrink back from the demands and benefits of the Cross.

> [5] But he was wounded for our transgressions, he was bruised for our iniquities: the chastisement of our peace was upon him; and with his stripes we are healed. [6] All we like sheep have gone astray; we have turned everyone to his own way; and the Lord hath laid on him the iniquity of us all. [7] He was oppressed, and he was afflicted, yet he opened not his mouth: he is brought as a lamb to the slaughter, and as a sheep before her shearers is dumb, so he openeth not his mouth. [8] He was taken from prison and from judgment: and who shall declare his generation? for he was cut off out of the land of the living: for the transgression of my people was he stricken. [9] And he made his grave with the wicked, and with the rich in his death; because he had done no violence, neither was any deceit in his mouth. [10] Yet it pleased the Lord to bruise him; he hath put him to grief: when thou shalt make his soul an offering for sin, he shall see his seed, he shall prolong his days, and the pleasure of the Lord shall prosper in his hand. [11] He shall see of the travail of his soul, and shall be satisfied: by his knowledge shall my righteous servant justify many; for he shall bear their iniquities. [12] Therefore will I divide him a portion with the great, and he shall divide the spoil with the strong; because he hath poured out his soul unto death: and he was numbered with the transgressors; and he bare the sin of many, and made intercession for the transgressors. (Isaiah 53:5-12, KJV).

Contained in Isaiah Chapter 53 are multiple prophecies pertaining to what the Messiah would do and what would be done to the Messiah. Jesus fulfilled all of them proving that He is the Messiah. All our sins were laid upon and borne by Jesus and He was led as a lamb to the slaughter. The slaughter took place on the Cross. Christ fulfilled the Isaiah 53 prophecy by dying for the ungodly. Very rarely will anyone die for a righteous man, though for a good man someone might possibly dare to die. God demonstrated His own love for us in this: While we were still sinners, Christ died for us. (Romans 5:6-8, KJV).

Regarding the death of Christ, it was also prophesied in the Old Testament that the Messiah would be mocked and ridiculed.

All they that see me laugh me to scorn: they shoot out the lip, they shake the head, saying, He trusted on the Lord that He will deliver Him, seeing He delighted in Him. (Psalm 22:7-8, KJV). This was fulfilled by Jesus as evidenced in the New Testament where the soldiers also mocked Him at His crucifixion, and where the rulers and the people also derided Him. They had mocked Him saying, He saved others; let Him save Himself, if He be Christ, the chosen of God (Luke 23:35-36, KJV).

Also in Psalm 22:18, it was prophesied that the garments of the Messiah would be divided and that lots would be cast for His clothing. Matthew 27:35 records the crucifixion of Jesus Christ: And they crucified Him, and parted His garments, casting lots: that it might be fulfilled which was spoken by the prophet, They parted My garments among them, and upon My vesture did they cast lots.

There are so many other Old Testament prophecies that point to the Cross of Christ because the Cross is at the foundation of our Christian faith. Isaiah 53:12 prophesied that Jesus will be crucified with criminals. Matthew 27:38 records that two thieves were crucified with Jesus the Christ, one on the right hand and the other on the left. In Psalm 22:16 and Zechariah 12:10 it was prophesied that the Messiah's hands and feet would be pierced. In John 20:25-27, when Jesus appeared to the doubting apostle Thomas after His resurrection, Jesus presented him with evidence of the piercings.

The plan of God was that the Messiah would take upon Himself the sins of the world so that those that believe would receive the righteousness of the Messiah in exchange. As a result of the Messiah taking upon Himself our sins, God visited the punishment for our sins upon the Messiah. As such, it was prophesied in Psalm 22:1 that God would forsake the Messiah and not save Him on the Cross. Matthew 27:46 in recording the fulfillment of this prophecy in Psalm 22:1 states: And about the ninth hour Jesus cried with a loud voice, saying, Eli, Eli, lama sabachthani? that is to say, My God, My God, why hast Thou forsaken Me?

In addition to all this, it was prophesied that the Messiah would demonstrate His agape love by praying for His enemies while He was enduring the agony of the Cross. In Psalm 109:4, David prophesied: 'For my love they are my adversaries: but I give myself unto prayer. Luke 23:34 narrates part of the events at the crucifixion as follows: 'Then said Jesus, Father, forgive them; for they know not what they do. And they parted His raiment, and cast lots.'

The Messianic prophecies point to the death of Christ which took place on the Cross. The good news is that Christ did not remain in death, but He rose from death on the third day. The resurrection further established the deity of Jesus Christ the Messiah. The prayer of king David in Psalm 16:9-10 gives us a hint of Christ's resurrection.

> Therefore my heart is glad, and my glory rejoiceth: my flesh also shall rest in hope. For thou will not leave my soul in hell, neither wilt thou suffer thine Holy One to see corruption. (Psalm 16:9-10, KJV).

In the course of Jesus' earthly ministry, He spoke of His dying and His coming back to life on the third day.

> From that time forth began Jesus to show unto his disciples, how that he must go unto Jerusalem, and suffer many things of the elders and chief priests and scribes, and be killed, and be raised again the third day. (Matthew 16:21, KJV).

Jesus demonstrated His resurrection power by bringing back the daughter of a ruler of the synagogue, named Jairus, back to life. Jesus introduced Himself as the Resurrection and the Life in John 11 when He called forth Lazarus from the grave. By His resurrection, Jesus confirmed that He is the author of life and that we are assured of eternal life. Without the crucifixion, there could be no resurrection.

THE SIGNIFICANCE OF THE CROSS OF CHRIST

An altar is a place or structure where religious rites are performed or on which sacrifices are offered to gods, idols, deities, or ancestors. In the Old Testament, God established an altar for Himself. The altar of the Lord is holy. Even though an altar is primarily a place of sacrifice, it has other functions and serves other purposes. As we shall see subsequently, the Cross of Christ is an altar. In fact, the Cross of Christ is the greatest altar there ever was and that there ever would be.

The Cross as an Altar of Prayer

In Exodus 30, God instructs Moses to build an altar of acacia wood to burn incense upon. The altar was to be overlaid with pure gold. The altar of the Lord is holy and has tremendous value. To communicate the spiritual value of this altar, God asked Moses to overlay it with gold. God commanded that no strange incense be burnt at this altar. However in Numbers 3:4, we read that Nadab and Abihu the sons of Aaron died before the Lord, when they offered strange fire before the Lord in the wilderness of Sinai. The sons of Aaron did not follow God's rule but decided to do their own thing. The incense that the two sons of Aaron burnt was contrary to God's word. Prior to the disobedience of Aaron's son, Moses and Aaron had offered the right burnt offering unto the Lord. The fire comes from God and not man. God can never be pleased with man-made fire offered up on the altar of His sanctuary.

> And Moses and Aaron went into the tabernacle of the congregation, and came out, and blessed the people: and the glory of the Lord appeared unto all the people. And there came a fire out from before the Lord, and consumed upon the altar the burnt offering and the fat: which when all the people saw, they shouted and fell on their faces. (Leviticus 9:23-24, KJV).

> And Nadab and Abihu, the sons of Aaron, took either of them his censer, and put fire therein, and put incense thereon, and offered strange fire before the Lord, which he

commanded them not. And there went out fire from the Lord, and devoured them, and they died before the Lord. (Leviticus 10:1-2, KJV).

In the above-mentioned Scriptures, one fire that came from the Lord consumed the burnt offering. The other fire that came from the Lord consumed the two persons that offered a strange fire. They died before the Lord. Many churches offering strange fire have died before the Lord. In the sight of man, just like the church in Sardis, they have a reputation of being alive. But before God, they are dead. However, and thankfully, God is a Restorer Who resurrects dead things. Churches in this unfortunate state need to repent and come back to their first love, Jesus Christ.

A circle of churches that have been praying for their human enemies to fall down and die, contrary to God's word to love their enemies, will need to seriously re-think their approach in light of God's Word. They are offering strange fire on the altar of God. It is God that prescribed the use of fire at the altar of incense. It was not man's idea. The fire in the Old Testament was a shadow of the divided tongues of fire to be received at Pentecost. It pointed to the Spirit of Prayer and Supplication, the baptism of the Holy Spirit and fire. Before God, only holy fire is acceptable. Nowadays, so many strange tongues and strange baptisms are ministering upon the altars of the Lord.

In Psalm 138:2, God makes it clear that He has exalted His Word above His name. God gives more honor to His Word than to even His own name. His Word is His integrity and character at stake. God's Word means more to Him than His power or reputation. God will refrain from exercising power if it goes against His Word. Many churches are offering strange prayers at God's altars. They are not following the prescribed pattern that God set for the worship that is due unto Him. Some of our prayers have become an abomination to the Lord simply because some of these prayers contradict His Word. Unauthorized persons, many of whom may not even be in Christ, have captured God's altars to offer strange prayers. God had chosen the Prophet Samuel as the one to offer a burnt offering unto Him. As is the case with some ministering from God's altars today, king Saul hijacked Samuel's office and conducted the burnt offering unto the Lord. God rejected what Saul did and punished Saul for it. God will always reject whatever He has not commanded no matter how impressive it may seem in the eyes of man. King Saul, instead of submitting to God's Word, put himself above God's Word and did things his own way.

Many of our modern-day churches are under the influence of the spirits of pride and competition. Pride is a desire to show that you are better than others. It is a feeling of elevated self-importance. The spirit of pride has caused many churches to think that they are the only ones that matter in the spiritual space. They engage in self-promotion and the promotion of man even when they offer prayers from God's altar. This is strange fire that God will not accept. Then there is the spirit of competition. Churches must not view other churches as rivals. Churches must not compete for membership, and must not compete for attention. This spirit is akin to an Absalom spirit that wanted to compete against his father for the kingship of Israel. We have witnessed an increase in men of God publicly attacking one another in order to show that they are more relevant. God is grieved when the Church lets in a spirit of competition and pride. Sometimes, this is evident by their praying in such a manner that God should make them bigger or richer than the church next door. They may not pray so outwardly, but God looks at the heart. Getting our churches back to Christ will require that we revisit our altars of prayers. The body of believers must be truly broken before the Lord. To show how important God views His altar, Jesus gives His followers an instruction. He tells them that when they know a brother has something against them, they must leave their gift at the altar and go settle the matter first with their brother. Afterwards, they can present the gift at the altar. Otherwise, that gift would be a strange gift on God's altar. God's altar is holy. It is a place for praying prayers that are in consonance with the will of God.

> Then said Jesus, Father, forgive them; for they know not
> what they do. And they parted his raiment, and cast lots.
> (Luke 23:34, KJV).

While offering Himself as a sacrifice for sin on the Cross, Jesus found time to pray on the Cross for the forgiveness of those that were hurting Him. He prayed for the forgiveness of His enemies from the Cross. The Cross is an altar. Jesus did not pursue the downfall of His enemies while He hung on the Cross. A few churches today have gotten so wrapped up in praying against human enemies. If you sincerely pray for God to forgive your enemies just like Christ did, then you would no longer seek their destruction. The church must go back to the place where we sincerely love our enemies. This is evidence of Christlikeness.

The Cross as an Altar of Sacrifice

The Old Testament spelt out the sacrificial system of worship in elaborate details. God was the first person that sacrificed an animal to cover the nakedness of Adam and Eve that resulted from their sinning. As time progressed God began to teach man the spiritual significance of an altar of sacrifice. The sacrifice had to be of a particular nature and quality and be made upon the altar that was prescribed. In the course of the Old Testament, man brought lambs, goats, bulls, and other animals to sacrifice before the Lord. In the New Testament, God brought His One and Only begotten Son to sacrifice on the Cross for the sins of the whole world. This was an all sufficient sacrifice done once and for all. We must appreciate the value of the Cross as the prophesied and prescribed place for the sacrifice of Christ. This is what makes the Cross the most potent altar of all altars on earth. The Cross is not to be deified as some have suggested. Deifying the Cross of Christ will only elevate it to the status of an idol. God is not pleased with idolatry. Sacrifice is extremely important to God. It means a lot to Him. It shows worship, repentance, love, and commitment toward Him. Mere religiosity, such as wearing a cross upon one's neck, is of no significance if our lives do not honor the Christ of the Cross. An interesting Scripture is tucked away in Hosea 8:11.

> Because Ephraim had made many altars to sin, altars shall
> be unto him to sin. (Hosea 8:11, KJV).

Ephraim had exhibited much disregard for the law of God. They sought to cover up their disobedience by building many altars to the Lord. The altars they built became a snare unto them. Ephraim hardened their hearts and depended solely on their altars for salvation. Their sin offerings upon their altars were in vain. Worship without obedience is in vain. The body of Christ must be careful not to fall into the convenience of honoring God with our lips while our hearts are far away from Him. The Cross of Christ does not save. Rather, it is the Christ of the Cross that saves. The Cross is the venue and the altar upon which Salvation (Jesus Christ) was given to man.

In Psalm 50:5, God calls for His consecrated ones, those that had made a covenant with Him by sacrifice.

In Genesis 22, God tested Abraham. Till today, God still tests man. He tries the reins of our hearts to see what we are made of. God still tests His church. Jesus sent messages to the seven churches of Asia Minor. Some of them he had weighed on the scale and found wanting. In Genesis 22, it was time for Abraham, described as the father of our faith, to be tested. God told Abraham to take his only son, Isaac, that he loved, and go to the region of Moriah. God instructed Abraham to sacrifice Isaac there on one of the mountains that He will tell him about. Note that the sacrifice was to take place at a certain region and on a particular mountain to be revealed. Abraham obeyed God and took Isaac to the region of Moriah. He set Isaac up as a burnt offering unto the Lord. Isaac was bewildered and wondered where the lamb to be sacrificed was. Just like Christ that was to come much later, Isaac did not raise his voice and was willing to be slaughtered. Just like God the Father that gave up His only begotten Son, Abraham also was willing to do likewise. Abraham demonstrated his willingness to obey God by not withholding Isaac. For this reason, God pronounced a great blessing upon Abraham. How many churches today are willing to give up their most prized earthly possession for the cause of Christ? The local churches must demonstrate this kind of selflessness that Abraham demonstrated. The test before Abraham was to choose between God and his most valuable possession, Isaac. For faith to be trusted, it must be tested. Abraham passed the test. Abraham showed that he did not love the gift (Isaac) more than the giver of the gift (God). Eventually, God provided a lamb in place of Isaac. Abraham then sacrificed that lamb as a burnt offering instead of his son. That lamb took the place of Isaac. That lamb, symbolically, took the place of man. God did provide Christ as an offering for sin.

The book of Leviticus deals with Old Testament forms of worship and prescribes how a sinner can enter the presence of God. Leviticus lays down the order of worship in the presence of God. In Leviticus 16, Aaron the high priest could only enter the holy place with a young bullock for a sin offering, and a ram for a burnt offering. If he entered otherwise, he would have died. In addition, from the Israelite community, Aaron was to take two male goats for a sin offering and a ram for a burnt offering. By the casting of lots, one of the goats was given as a sin offering unto the Lord. The other was to be a scapegoat which would be presented before the Lord alive. The scapegoat was used to make an atonement before the Lord, and then released into the wilderness. This ritual that God commanded to be performed, among other requirements, had spiritual implications. The rituals conveyed a message pointing to Jesus Christ. The goat that was offered as a sin offering reminded the people that sin demanded death as a penalty. The question then was: Who would pay the price? John the Baptist answered this question in John1:29 and John 1:36: "And looking upon Jesus as he walked, he saith,

Behold the Lamb of God!" In Old Testament times, the sacrificed goat perished as a sin offering. The scapegoat took away the people's impurities and sins into the wilderness. Both goats symbolized Christ. Both goats paid the penalty for the people's sins by being their substitute. The sins were imputed to the goats. However, because of the finished work of Christ on the Cross of Calvary, animal sacrifices are no longer required for the propitiation, the covering of our sins. Jesus Christ is the ultimate and perfect sacrifice. (John 1:29). Jesus is the Lamb of God that takes away the sins of the world. God made Christ who had no sin to be sin for us, so that in Christ we might become the righteousness of God. (2 Corinthians 5:21).

In the spirit realm, sacrifices take place at designated altars. In the kingdom of darkness, sacrifices are made to Satan and other false gods at designated altars. These are demonic altars. On the other hand, the Cross of Christ is an altar of righteousness. God looks at the quality of our sacrifice. He gave us His best in the person of Jesus Christ. God wants to know that our churches in these end times will not withhold their best from Him. He wants us to be willing to always present our best just as Abraham did with Isaac. God rebuked the priests in the time of the Prophet Malachi for not offering their best to Him.

> [6] A son honoreth his father, and a servant his master: if then I be a father, where is mine honor? and if I be a master, where is my fear? saith the Lord of hosts unto you, O priests, that despise my name. And ye say, Wherein have we despised thy name? [7] Ye offer polluted bread upon mine altar; and ye say, Wherein have we polluted thee? In that ye say, The table of the Lord is contemptible. [8] And if ye offer the blind for sacrifice, is it not evil? and if ye offer the lame and sick, is it not evil? offer it now unto thy governor; will he be pleased with thee, or accept thy person? saith the Lord of hosts. [9] And now, I pray you, beseech God that he will be gracious unto us: this hath been by your means: will he regard your persons? saith the Lord of hosts. [10] Who is there even among you that would shut the doors for nought? neither do ye kindle fire on mine altar for nought. I have no pleasure in you, saith the Lord of hosts, neither will I accept an offering at your hand. (Malachi 1:6-10, KJV).

An altar of sacrifice speaks of death. The Cross speaks of death. At the Cross, a righteous man was slain for the sins of the unrighteous. To live is Christ and to die is gain. Members of the body of Christ must be willing to offer themselves up to God as a living sacrifice. To do so, we must become selfless. We must be willing to sacrifice all. A church that is not willing to get her hands dirty to make others clean is a church that seeks to serve the Lord only when it is convenient. God often works with those that are willing to give their all for the cause of Christ. This was the problem the rich young ruler encountered with Christ in Luke 18. He wanted to hold on to his most prized possessions and serve Christ. In effect, he was saying that he could not serve Christ unconditionally. Many today are like this rich young ruler. They value their wealth, their status, their privileges, and their lives more than they value Christ. Christ only has meaning to them so long as they have these worldly things. They have not been to the Cross to offer themselves up to die. In Luke 9:23, Jesus said that if any man will come after Him, that man must deny himself, and take up his cross daily, and follow Him. While we need money to run our churches and to preach the gospel all over the world, the Church must not place its confidence in money. The Church must be willing to sacrifice money for God and not sacrifice God for money.

The Spirit of the Lord is saying to the churches in these end times, "Can you be like my servant, Job? A perfect and an upright man, one that feareth God, and escheweth evil?" (Job 1:8, KJV). God considered Job blameless. Christ could not say the same for five of the seven churches in the book of Revelation. Job feared God. Many churches these days lack the fear of God and so have become their own god.

The Cross as an Altar of Exchange

An altar is also a place of exchange. Even at the altars of the heathen of the world, exchanges take place. Blood sacrifices are made in exchange for some perceived advantage from a deity. Fertility gods required sacrifices upon altars in their temples. The heathen give sacrifices to their gods in exchange for some perceived favor, such as wealth, fame, position, or fertility.

The altars of the Lord are holy. A holy altar can be profaned by the wrong sacrifice. God is displeased when the wrong sacrifice is placed on His altar. Instead of commendation, He will offer a rebuke. More importantly,

God is displeased when we treat His own sacrifice in the person of Christ with disrespect. An altar is a place of exchange. Christ was offered up on the altar of the Cross in exchange for our souls. We gave Him our bad and took His good. This took place on the Cross when He died a sacrificial death for our sins.

> For ye know the grace of our Lord Jesus Christ, that, though he was rich, yet for your sakes he became poor, that ye through his poverty might be rich. (2 Corinthians 8:9, KJV).

> For he hath made him to be sin for us, who knew no sin; that we might be made the righteousness of God in him. (2 Corinthians 5:21, KJV).

These Scriptures relate to an exchange that took place. This exchange was only made possible by Jesus dying on the Cross. Jesus had to shed His blood on the Cross for us to receive His righteousness by faith.

> Come unto me, all ye that labor and are heavy laden, and I will give you rest. (Matthew 11:28, KJV).

In exchange for our coming to Christ and our abiding in Christ, Christ gives us rest. Rest covers peace, satisfaction, salvation, and victory. All these things were made possible because the Lamb of God was willing to go to the Cross and die for our sakes. We have so much to receive from Christ in exchange for our sacrificing our lives for Him. We sacrifice our lives by denying ourselves and taking up our crosses to follow Him. Our churches have barely scratched the surface in receiving all that Christ has for us. His riches are unsearchable. (Ephesians 3:8).

The Cross as an Altar of Covenant

Often times, oaths and covenants are made at altars. The New Covenant (New Testament) was made on the Cross and sealed with the blood of Jesus.

In Genesis 15, God established a covenant with Abraham. God told Abraham to bring a heifer, a goat, and a ram, each three years old, along with a dove and a young pigeon. Abraham brought all these to God as instructed and cut them in two and arranged them opposite each other. The birds however, he did not cut in half. Abraham then fell into a deep sleep, and a thick and dreadful darkness came over him. God then told Abraham how his descendants will be slaves four hundred years in a foreign land. Thereafter, a smoking furnace and a burning lamp appeared and passed between the animal pieces. The Bible states in Genesis 15:18, KJV, that on that day, God made a covenant with Abraham giving him and his descendants the land of Canaan. This covenant was preceded by a sacrifice. The smoking furnace and burning lamp that went between the pieces was a representation of God's divine presence.

The New Covenant in Christ was established on the Cross. Since Christ on the Cross could not have the last supper on the Cross evidencing the new covenant, He had that last supper prior to His crucifixion. At the last supper, which the body of Christ celebrates as the Eucharist or Holy Communion, the new covenant was established in reference to Christ's blood that was to be shed on the Cross.

> 23 For I have received of the Lord that which also I delivered unto you, that the Lord Jesus the same night in which he was betrayed took bread: 24 And when he had given thanks, he brake it, and said, Take, eat: this is my body, which is broken for you: this do in remembrance of me. 25 After the same manner also he took the cup, when he had supped, saying, this cup is the new testament in my blood: this do ye, as oft as ye drink it, in remembrance of me. 26 For as often as ye eat this bread, and drink this cup, ye do shew the Lord's death till he come. (1 Corinthians 11:23-26, KJV).

It was almost as if Christ held a memorial service for Himself while He was still alive. Christ broke the bread and told them it was His body which was to be broken for them. He took the cup of wine and shared among His apostles telling them that as often as they drink the wine and eat the bread, they should do so in remembrance of Him. This was on the eve of His betrayal. Later on, Christ was crucified on the Cross where He sealed this covenant with His blood. It is the blood of Jesus that was shed on the Cross of Calvary that gives the believer life. The life is in the blood. As we appropriate the blood of Jesus, we must always remember and appreciate the sacrifice He made for us on the Cross. At the Cross, Christ said, "It is finished". His earthly ministry on earth was completed. He had redeemed man from sin by making a new covenant in His blood.

The Cross as an Altar of Warfare

In the Old Testament, in the course of a battle, we sometimes see sacrifices being made on an altar to enhance the outcome of the war. Israel and Moab were at war. In the course of the battle, Moab had suffered some severe setbacks. When the king of Moab saw that the battle was going against him, he took his firstborn son, who was to succeed him as king, and offered him as a sacrifice on the city wall. This elevated Moab's hatred and wrath against Israel. This, in turn, caused Israel to leave the scene disgusted at what they saw. (2 kings 3:27).

The greatest victory on earth was won on the Cross by Jesus Christ. The spiritual warfare that Christ fought on the Cross disarmed Satan.

> But we speak the wisdom of God in a mystery, even the hidden wisdom, which God ordained before the world unto our glory: Which none of the princes of this world knew: for had they known it, they would not have crucified the Lord of glory. (1 Corinthians 2:7-8, KJV).

God gave up Christ for the sins of the world. By crucifying Christ, Satan not only shot himself in the foot; Satan shot himself in the head. Christ won the victory for Christians on the Cross.

> Blotting out the handwriting of ordinances that was against us, which was contrary to us, and took it out of the way, nailing it to his Cross, And having spoiled principalities and powers, he made a show of them openly, triumphing over them in it. (Colossians 2:14-15).

> [7] And there was war in heaven: Michael and his angels fought against the dragon; and the dragon fought and his angels, [8] And prevailed not; neither was their place found

any more in heaven.m[9] And the great dragon was cast out, that old serpent, called the Devil, and Satan, which deceiveth the whole world: he was cast out into the earth, and his angels were cast out with him. [10] And I heard a loud voice saying in heaven, Now is come salvation, and strength, and the kingdom of our God, and the power of his Christ: for the accuser of our brethren is cast down, which accused them before our God day and night. [11] And they overcame him by the blood of the Lamb, and by the word of their testimony; and they loved not their lives unto the death. (Revelation 12:7-11, KJV).

In the battle against evil, the finished work of Christ on the Cross prevailed. It is by the finished work of Christ on the Cross that all our victories are won.

Glorying in the Cross

In these end times, it is critical that all churches return to the Christ of the Cross. The apostle Paul gloried in the Cross of Christ. He did not glory in how many converts he won to Christ or in how successful he was. But God forbid that I should glory, save in the Cross of our Lord Jesus Christ, by whom the world is crucified unto me, and I unto the world. (Galatians 6:14). When Paul wrote his first letter to the church in Corinth, he wrote to reconcile them. They had become a divided church. Apostle Paul made it clear that he was determined not to know anything among them, except Jesus Christ, and Him crucified. (1 Corinthians 2:2). Believers need to get back to glorying in the Cross of Christ and not in the things of the world. The past few decades have seen a rise in churches preaching more prosperity and more miracles. They have gloried in prosperity but not in the Cross of Jesus Christ. The Cross of Jesus Christ will demand that you crucify your flesh. While many are burning both ends of the candle to acquire more alabaster boxes, Jesus is watching for who will break an alabaster box for Him. The spirit of worldliness that has stormed many of the local churches has resulted in believers not living close to the Cross. Rather, many believers are pre-occupied with vanities. The Cross will demand that you fast, and that you deny yourself. The Cross will crucify the flesh and pave the way for you to walk in the Spirit. A believer that glories in the Cross is less likely to be allured by the pleasures of the world. A believer that is crucified unto the world and whom the world is crucified unto is one that will produce the fruit of the Spirit. The life of such a believer flows with love, joy, peace, long-suffering, gentleness, goodness, faith, meekness, and temperance. Against such characteristics, there is no law. The Cross leads us to a place of brokenness. The Church must return to glorying in the Cross. The Cross points to humility and tranquilizes pride. Christ humbled Himself and became obedient unto death, even the death of the Cross. For this reason, God exalted Him, and gave Christ a name that is above every name. (Philippians 2:8-9).

The problem we face today is that many want the Christ but do not want His Cross. They want a Christ that will do for them, and not a Christ that will demand from them. The Cross demands the greatest thing that you have to offer. It demands your life. There is a price for following Christ. The Church must always be willing to pay that price, no matter the cost. Many Christians, and many churches are living for themselves. We must avoid the temptation to be all about only our own agenda. Some have taken heavy loans and are now unable to repay their debts. They may have become entangled in projects that Christ may not have approved of. The Cross will teach you how to cut your coat according to your size. This is why many do not embrace Christ's Cross. The Cross leads to a place of self-denial, and self-sacrifice. The Cross demands submission. Christ submitted to death on the Cross. A true disciple of Christ devotes all that he has to Christ. He does not cling to anything except the old rugged Cross.

> For many walk of whom I have told you often, and now tell
> you even weeping, that they are the enemies of the Cross
> of Christ. (Philippians 3:18, KJV).

Paul calls many the enemies of the Cross of Christ. He does not refer to them as the enemies of Christ. In other words, they want a Christ without a Cross. They worship Christ mainly for what they can get. They shy away from the Christ of the Bible that demands that they walk on the straight and narrow way. The straight and narrow way is the way of the Cross. These are not true Christians because they are not willing to lay down their lives on the Cross. They only profess Christ for the sake of earthly things. You cannot glory in Christ Jesus apart from His Cross. Many of the churches of the previous centuries that endorsed, or maintained a neutral stand, in the face of gross injustices perpetrated against humanity did not glory in the Cross of Christ. They kept silence in order to keep their privileged status. The Cross of Christ will demand your entitlements and privileges. Just like it did to Jesus, it will demand that you die to self so that others may live. Churches that only advance their self-interest are unwilling to sacrifice for the cause of Christ.

The churches that have prospered through a counterfeit gospel like the prosperity gospel do not glory in the Cross. It is the money that the prosperity gospel preachers are after. The gospel that keeps hounding people to "sow a seed", "name it and claim it", "believe it and receive it", and hardly teaches righteousness is a corrupted gospel. Many of the top prosperity gospel preachers can hardly bear the reproach of Christ. The only time they seem to suffer reproach is when they get caught for wrongdoing. There are some churches whose main message is that if you give a generous offering to their ministry you will receive a financial blessing. They have made prosperity the central theme of the gospel. The righteousness of Christ is the central theme of the gospel. Christ imparted His righteousness unto the believer on the Cross. He that knew no sin became sin for us that we might receive the righteousness of God in Christ. These prosperity gospel preachers in our midst have given the Christian faith a bad reputation. They are like those money changers in the temple that Christ chased out with a whip.

Christianity Today published an article in its September 7, 2019 online edition. The title of the article was: *Benny Hinn renounces His Selling of God's Blessings. Critics Want More.* In that article, Daniel Silliman wrote:

> Hinn said he now believes such give-to-get theology is offensive to God. He specifically repudiated the practice of asking for "seed money," where televangelists tell people that God will bless them if they give a specific dollar amount. Hinn himself has done this numerous times, promising God will give material blessings in exchange for a gift of $1,000.

Christianity Today had a cover story on July 6, 2007 which was titled: *Gospel Riches - Africa's Rapid Embrace of Prosperity Pentecostalism Provokes Concern and Hope.*

Bishop of the Redeemed Evangelical Mission (TREM) since 1988, Okonkwo presides over the annual Kingdom Life World Conference of 150 prosperity-oriented churches. But tonight he yields the podium to the Rev. Felix Omobude, who urges the crowd to dream big. "There are so many dream killers around," he says. "Don't let them kill your dream." Omobude prophesies: "Your tomorrow will be better than today. In 2007 you will take your place."

The crowd is thrilled. Omobude promises that women will find husbands, audience members will buy new cars, and the barren will birth twins. To open themselves to this blessing, Omobude encourages the crowd to give N25,000 (about $200). Local schoolteachers earn only $150 per month, so the amount is significant. Yet more than 300 people swarm Omobude, who rubs oil from a bowl on their palms. Within minutes, the church nets a tax-free $60,000.

The Church must return to the Cross of Christ. The idea of using money to buy God's favor does not align with the New Testament teachings of Jesus Christ. Jesus healed and delivered many that were poor. When He blessed the rich, He did not ask for anything. When the rich young ruler encountered Christ, Christ did not ask him for money. Rather, He asked him to sell all his possessions and give to the poor and then come follow Him. When God used the Prophet Elisha to heal Naaman of leprosy, Elisha refused the reward that Naaman offered him. Elisha's servant, Gehazi, went behind Elisha's back and took the reward for himself. The leprosy of Naaman fell on Gehazi. God is not moved by money. God is moved by your heart. Many false prosperity gospel preachers have used 1 Kings 3 where Solomon sacrificed a thousand burnt offerings to the Lord to claim that that provoked God to appear to Solomon in a dream and say to him to ask for whatever he desires. What moved God was not the sacrifice of Solomon. After all, Israel had given enormous sacrifices in the past that God rejected. God cannot be impressed with a thousand burnt offerings. What moved God to favor Solomon is found in 1 Kings 3:3, KJV: And Solomon loved the Lord, walking in the statutes of David his father: only he sacrificed and burnt incense in high places. Solomon loved the Lord. If you do not love the

Lord and you give God a big "seed" offering, God will not be impressed. Giving to get is born by a spirit of greed. The churches that are propagating this false teachings on prosperity need to repent and return to Christ. They need to glory in nothing else but the Cross of Christ. For if we suffer with Christ, we shall reign with Him. The Cross is the place of suffering. It is also the place of salvation, healing, deliverance, reconciliation, and victory. No crucifixion, no resurrection. No death, no life.

CHAPTER FIVE

DIVISIONS, DENOMINATIONALISM, AND THE ECUMENICAL MOVEMENT

"If there is no God, everything is permissible."
Fyodor Dostoevsky

The unity of man was fragmented at the fall of man in the garden of Eden. Adam shied away from taking responsibility for his disobedience and subtly tried to put the blame on God and the woman that God gave him. Man's unity was further fractured when Cain refused to be his brother's keeper. Driven by a spirit of rivalry and anger, Cain murdered Abel. At the tower of Babel, man's unity was further broken as each man received a new language and did not understand the other.

When Jesus came on the scene, He made it clear that His work would bring division. (Matthew 10:34-36). Many would be opposed to His work. His work involved calling out a people from the world unto Himself. The ones He was calling out from the world unto Himself - the Ecclesia, the Church - would be one and undivided. They would not be characterized by the divisions that plague the world. They would be united in Him.

Jesus Christ is the foundation and builder of the Church. In Jesus' high priestly prayer in John 17, He prayed that the Church would be one.

> 20 "I do not pray for these alone, but also for those who [j]
> will believe in Me through their word; 21 that they all may
> be one, as You, Father, *are* in Me, and I in You; that they
> also may be one in Us, that the world may believe that
> You sent Me. 22 And the glory which You gave Me I have
> given them, that they may be one just as We are one: (John
> 17:20-22, NKJV).

Unfortunately, the Church, throughout her history, has experienced so much strife and division in her ranks. The division has cut across issues of dogma, idiosyncrasies, and ecclesiastical governance. It seems like the Church is divided on almost every issue. A divided house can never reach its full potential. In an attempt to cure these divisions, some have proposed a fusion of doctrines and practices. For any such proposition, no matter how well intentioned, to stand, it must be subjected to biblical scrutiny. Generally speaking, the Christian faith is averse to conflict from within. However, often times, it has been through some of these conflicts that growth has been experienced.

Church Division in Bible Times

The Church of Jesus Christ was established at Pentecost by the Holy Spirit in Acts 2. The Bible records that the disciples were all together in one accord. There was no strife or division among them. As the Church began to grow, disputes began to arise. In Acts 6, a dispute arose regarding fairness in the daily distribution of food among the widows. This kind of dispute can easily be resolved. The more challenging disputes the Church faces within its rank concerns matters of doctrinal interpretation. It is more difficult to reconcile differences in dogma and doctrine than it is to resolve a quarrel over food. Nonetheless, the minutest of quarrels, if not well addressed, has the potential to divide the body of Christ.

> And in those days, when the number of the disciples was
> multiplied, there arose a murmuring of the Grecians
> against the Hebrews, because their widows were neglected
> in the daily ministration. 2 Then the twelve called the
> multitude of the disciples unto them, and said, It is not

reason that we should leave the word of God, and serve tables. ³Wherefore, brethren, look ye out among you seven men of honest report, full of the Holy Ghost and wisdom, whom we may appoint over this business. ⁴But we will give ourselves continually to prayer, and to the ministry of the word. ⁵And the saying pleased the whole multitude: and they chose Stephen, a man full of faith and of the Holy Ghost, and Philip, and Prochorus, and Nicanor, and Timon, and Parmenas, and Nicolas a proselyte of Antioch: ⁶Whom they set before the apostles: and when they had prayed, they laid their hands on them. (Acts 6:1-6, KJV).

In Acts 6, the early church in Jerusalem had the Grecians and the Hebrews, who, despite having the same Lord as fellow Jewish believers – with one group speaking Greek and the other Aramaic, respectively – saw themselves as separate people as soon as injustice and discrimination was perceived. It became somewhat of a "Them" versus "Us". The apostles knew their priorities to be the Word of God and prayer. Therefore, they delegated responsibilities to a new cadre of leadership: church deacons. The deacons provide support to the pastors so that the latter can focus on the word of God and prayer. Matters that do not relate to exegesis, church dogmas, scriptural doctrines, or ecclesiastical law can easily be delegated to the deacons. The deacons serve to ensure order and fairness in the Church. Their service is quite important in maintaining an atmosphere of cordiality and trust within the Church. However, it is not personal conflicts that have caused churches to divide along denominational lines. The rupture often took place when differences in interpretation of Scripture, doctrines, and dogmas could not be reconciled. Such was the case in Acts 15. It took the intervention of the apostles at the Jerusalem Council to avoid this.

In Acts 15, a doctrinal issue arose that had the potential of dividing the Church. The issue was whether circumcision was necessary for salvation. Certain men had come from Judea to the church in Antioch and were teaching the believers at Antioch that except they were circumcised according to the custom of Moses, they could not be saved. Paul and Barnabas rejected this teaching and so a dispute arose regarding the relevance of circumcision to salvation. This dispute was referred to the apostles in Jerusalem for determination. The apostles and elders in

Jerusalem came together to consider this matter. In the course of much disputing, Apostle Peter rose up to speak.

> [6] Now the apostles and elders came together to consider this matter. [7] And when there had been much dispute, Peter rose up *and* said to them: "Men *and* brethren, you know that a good while ago God chose among us, that by my mouth the Gentiles should hear the word of the gospel and believe. [8] So God, who knows the heart, acknowledged them by giving them the Holy Spirit, just as *He did* to us, [9] and made no distinction between us and them, purifying their hearts by faith. [10] Now therefore, why do you test God by putting a yoke on the neck of the disciples which neither our fathers nor we were able to bear? [11] But we believe that through the grace of the Lord Jesus Christ we shall be saved in the same manner as they." (Acts 16:6-11, KJV).

Apostle James agreed with Peter and resolved that a stumbling block should not be put in the way of the Gentiles that were turning to Christ. Peter made it clear that salvation was for all people and involved receiving the Holy Spirit. The Holy Spirit was not an exclusive gift to the Jews. He had also been poured out on the Gentiles. God's salvation for all people is by grace through faith and nothing more. Imposing other conditions such as circumcision strays away from God's plan of salvation. In similar vein, any church denomination requiring membership as a prerequisite for salvation, will be contradicting the Word of God. Thus, James concluded that a letter should be written to the church in Antioch, instructing the Gentiles there to abstain from things polluted by idols, from sexual immorality, from things strangled, and from blood. In reaching this right decision, the apostles and elders at Jerusalem were able to prevent the church at Antioch from imposing the customs of the Jews over the Gentiles. Churches have experienced division when customs and traditions have been given prominence above the gospel message of Christ. When customs and cultural patterns are adhered to in churches, the believers that do not belong to that custom or culture feel excluded from the body. The body of Christ is not a body of customs and traditions. It is the body of Christ. The body of the Word. The body of the Spirit of God; and where the Spirit of God is, there is liberty. The admission of human traditions into the Church invariably leads to bondage. In Galatians 2, Paul refers to the incident in Acts 15 where the false brethren came in unawares to spy out their liberty in Christ with a view to returning them to bondage. This type of conflict strikes at the heart of the gospel and could easily cause a church to split up. The spirit of error usually operates to introduce deception, and then contention, into the body of Christ. Contention has the potential to birth all manner of divisions and separations.

In Paul's letter to the Corinthian church, he addressed their schisms and divisions that were tearing the church apart. The members needed to see themselves not as individuals but as part of a body. Simon Peter informed the believers that were scattered throughout the regions of Galatia, Asia, and other parts that they were living stones being built up into a spiritual house. (1 Peter 2:5). As living stones, believers are connected one to another to form a spiritual house. We are one. The church in Corinth needed to understand that this spirit of oneness is contrary to the spirit of individualism. Paul did not mince words in setting them straight.

> And I, brethren, could not speak unto you as unto spiritual, but as unto carnal, even as unto babes in Christ. ² I have fed you with milk, and not with meat: for hitherto ye were not able to bear it, neither yet now are ye able. ³ For ye are yet carnal: for whereas there is among you envying, and strife, and divisions, are ye not carnal, and walk as men? ⁴ For while one saith, I am of Paul; and another, I am of Apollos; are ye not carnal? (1 Corinthians 3:1-4, KJV).

The church in Corinth, plagued with envying, strife, and divisions, allowed factions, carnality, and immaturity to divide them. For this, Paul reminded them how carnal they were. The church at Corinth was plagued with envying, strife, and divisions. Some said they were of Paul and some said they were of Apollos. The Church of God should not be divided along man's inclination toward his fellow man. The right attitude to foster oneness in our local churches is for all to understand that they are of Christ. The culture displayed in some churches where the parishioners are subservient to their pastors, and yet not submitted to Christ is indeed pitiable. While this may not necessarily lead to a divided church, it will eventually remove the focus from Christ and place it on a man. To be sure, it is right to give honor to a man where honor is due; moreover, the Bible admonishes us that the elders that rule well are worthy of double honor. (1 Timothy 5:17). However, the practice of man elevating man in a church setting, beyond what is appropriate, is an affront to the glory of God. For this reason, Paul was determined not to know anything among the Corinthians except Jesus Christ and Him crucified.

Christ is the Head of the body. Christ is not divided. The Head is one. The Church has one Lord, one faith, and one baptism. (Ephesians 4:5). Just as the Head is not divided, the body also should not be divided. Today's churches must remember that God has given Christ to be Head over all things to the Church. (Ephesians 1:22). A church that desires to return to a place where Christ is at the center of its being must not tolerate schisms within its ranks. The church must have effective mechanisms in place to deal with such schisms whenever they arise. The Church has not operated in its full power because of so many divisions. Who is dividing us and why? Most times, it is our flesh -old depraved, carnal nature- the great instrument of Satan. Satan is adept at dividing and conquering. For the Church to be more than a conqueror, it must go back to Christ. Satan has started wars not only *within* churches to divide them but also *between* churches to keep them from working together. The area where the Church as a body has been fragmented the most is in the area of denominationalism. In this area, owing to doctrine or some other reason, the division has been so acute that it resulted in one new church or other new churches coming out of the church they disagreed with. These new churches are not children of a parent church but rather splinter groups that claim no affiliation with the church from whence they emerged. In advocating for the Church's return to Christ, I began to see that our efforts will be worthless if we do not attempt to reconcile our denominations. How did these denominations arise and what purpose, if any, do they serve anyway?

Proliferation of Denominations

The uncountable denominations of Christianity point to a history of various splits in the body of Christ. The splits resulted in the formation of new groups of believers. Disagreement over beliefs and practices resulted in splinter groups bearing different names, and each claiming their position and authority from Christ. The rise of denominationalism has broken the organizational and structural unity of the body of Christ. The creation of each separate body seems to have encouraged more human arbitrariness in the church leadership. This has often been at variance with the leading of the Holy Spirit. The birth of denominations in Christianity is traceable to the Protestant works of Martin Luther in 1517. Martin Luther nailed his 95 Theses to the Wittenberg Castle church door in Germany protesting the doctrines and practices of the church of his day, the Roman Catholic Church. From that point on, denominations began to spring up. The works of Martin Luther resulted in a break away from the Catholic Church and resulted in the formation of the Protestant Church. From this breakaway, another group emerged in England, known as the Church of England - or the Anglican (Anglo-Canadian) Church. With this, began a fragmentation of the body of Christ. In the Netherlands, during the 1800s there was an exodus from the national church to form separate denominations. Often, these denominations succumbed to what they were supposedly against; and so new denominations emerged from within them. To compound matters, sub-denominations, quasi-denominations, and even pseudo-denominations, have arisen from the denominations. This is particularly so, in the Baptist denomination where there are so many sub-denominations, each going by the name Baptist but having no relationship with the initial Baptist denomination of the 17th century. As denominations continued to be birthed, the Church lost its power to speak with one voice.

The more denominations began to proliferate, the more urgent became the need for them to be regulated. With too many churches, there was bound to be confusion and a lack of accountability. And of course, government regulation of churches affected their independence. For instance, the Dutch National Reformed Church was by a Royal Decree in 1816 constituted as an establishment of the Monarchy in the Netherlands. Till today, it can be argued whether such a church owes its allegiance to the State or to Christ. Registration put the churches at a disadvantage. It gave them the status of an establishment under the good pleasure and graces of the government that registered it. No doubt, registration became necessary as some of the churches were inclined to abuse their status and power. Nonetheless, what is registered is not necessarily the Church of Christ in the spirit realm. Rather, it is a mere legal entity for purposes of the law. This legal entity, the church, is bound by Scripture to submit to the governmental authorities. As Christ educated Pontius Pilate, we also have learned that the governments of the earth have a measure of power over the churches because it was given to them from above.

Martin Luther can be said to have opened the flood gates to denominationalism. Once the gates were opened, the Church lost the power to close them. Since then, Christian denominations have grown in number, and in the thousands. The Protestants broke away from the Catholic Church as a result of the reformation brought about through Martin Luther. The two recognizable denominations of the time became the Catholic and the Protestant. As time progressed, the Protestant Church could not hold on to her unity; thus many other denominations began to flow out of her.

By the late 17th century, the Puritans, who had come out of the Protestant Reformation, sought to purify the Church with emphasis on holiness. From this group began a separation which brought about new denominations of Baptists, Presbyterians, and Quakers. England and America experienced a Great Awakening in the 18th century. From this Great Awakening came the birthing of other denominations, namely the Methodists and Wesleyans. It almost seemed that whenever there was a move of God that the old order did not embrace, a new denomination was founded. For instance, the AME, the African Methodist Episcopal denomination emerged out of the Methodist denomination in 1787. The AME arose when Richard Allen, a black American preacher walked out of St. George's Methodist Episcopal Church in Philadelphia, protesting against racism and racial discrimination. Richard Allen then founded the AME in 1794, a denomination in which blacks, regardless of status, could worship God freely. It was rather egregious to speak of a united Methodist church while racism was expressly endorsed by the ruling white clergy. The AME thus became the first Protestant denomination to be formed by black people. Sadly, among the denominations founded by blacks have arisen other black-dominated denominations, a few of which are centered upon the quest for a black Messiah. This attitude reduces God to the spirit of a nation or race. As was often the case, members of the new experience were not welcomed by their old established churches and found it difficult to remain there.

There is also the Seventh Day Adventist denomination that was birthed in the mid-1800s from the Second Great Awakening. In the course of the Second Great Awakening, a group of believers under one Baptist minister, William Miller strayed away from the Baptist Church. They were inspired by the false belief that the second advent of Christ would occur on October 22, 1844. To their disappointment, nothing of the sort occurred. Eventually, another prominent member of the Seventh Day Adventist denomination came up with another false revelation that Jesus still had work to do in the sanctuary, and so he decided to tarry. When denominations are formed based on the personal revelation of a leader, such disappointments, confusion, and error are bound to occur. Till today, the Seventh Day Adventist Church places more emphasis on the revelations and writings of one of her founders, Ellen G. White, than it does on Scripture. It also places emphasis on the strict observance of the Sabbath Day.

The latter part of the 19th century witnessed socio-economic, military, and colonial expansionism into new territories. This, in turn, caused many of the denominations to reconfigure their modes of outreach. The denominations began reconstituting themselves and taking on the form of corporate organizations. Becoming corporate enabled them to pursue their missionary ambitions abroad. It became common for the churches to now have church boards. The early churches in the book of Acts were not governed by church boards. Today, many church boards and boards of trustees may actually be standing in the way of a move of God. Most times, God is known to act through a man and not a committee.

In the 20th century, the Azusa Street Revival of 1906 through 1915 led by William Seymour, an African American preacher in California led to the Pentecostal movement. The Pentecostal denomination amplified the manifestation and power of the Holy Spirit and became the fastest growing denomination in America and around the world. From the Azusa Street Revival came the Pentecostal-Holiness Church, Assemblies of God (AG), and Church of God in Christ (COGIC). Pentecostals experienced a further split into Trinitarian Pentecostals and Unitarian (Oneness) Pentecostals over doctrinal differences relating to the trinity of God. In 1914, AG split from the African American dominated denomination of COGIC when 300 white preachers and many laymen met in Arkansas for that purpose. The AG is the largest Pentecostal denomination in the world today. From the Pentecostal fires of Azusa Street have come the birthing of thousands of denominations, all claiming Christ as Head but seeming to have a different body from the others. When an established church placed emphasis in a particular subject-matter of the Christian faith, another denomination would arise claiming that emphasis should be placed on something else. There is also the non-denominational church which many have argued, is also a denomination. It almost seems as if the Church by her behavior, has sanctioned a divisiveness that the Gospel has forbidden.

For instance, the Roman Catholics place a lot of emphasis on sacrament and tradition. The initial Protestants placed emphasis on the Word of God. Today, the Orthodox Church denominations place their emphasis on the liturgical ceremonial forms of worship. The Lutheran denomination, founded on the Protestant works of Martin Luther, is distinguished by its emphasis on the Scriptures and faith. The Presbyterians emphasize the sovereignty of God. The Baptists have as their emphasis, Scripture, conversion, and baptism. The Holiness Movement is driven by piety and separatism. The Pentecostal and Charismatic denominations emphasize the person and ministry of the Holy Spirit. African American church denominations, considering their history, tend to focus more on freedom, liberty, and restoration. Besides these aforementioned examples, there are so many other denominations with myriad variants and distinctions.

Another potent source of division within the body of Christ has been the issue of sex and sexuality. Some denominations like the Church of England (Anglican Communion) have endorsed same sex marriage and ordained homosexuals and lesbians as bishops, and church ministers. As a result of this, the Anglican Church of Nigeria, and some other African countries, broke away from the Church of England and thus became separate denominations. The Anglican Archbishop of Nigeria, Peter Akinola and his counterpart in Uganda, Archbishop Henry Luke, criticized the Anglican Church of England for accepting and ordaining gay priests. Archbishop Akinola made good his word that if England adopts a new faith, alien to what had been handed to them together, they will walk apart. This break away from the Church of England was significant considering that African countries make up roughly half of the population of Anglicans in the world. One group of the Anglican Church denomination sought to adapt to the sexual revolution, while another group in that denomination totally resisted it by remaining true to the Word of God. This disagreement led to the formation of a new denomination independent of the Anglican Church of England.

The sexual revolution has caused many unbelievers and believers alike to attack the stand of the Church. The stand of the Church has not been unequivocal. There have been cracks in the wall regarding where the Church stands in the unfolding sexual war for the minds and hearts of the people. This sexual revolution is a satanic agenda. The Word of God prohibits the sexual practices that the sexual revolution is promoting. The Bible calls homosexuality, lesbianism, and other forms of sexual perversion an abomination. Certain powerful sections of the media have aggressively pushed and advertised this satanic agenda that has only brought nothing but an astronomical explosion in abortions, fornication, adultery, divorce, lesbianism, homosexuality, teenage pregnancies, pornography, sexual abuse, increase in sexually transmitted diseases, and now same-sex marriages. The USA in particular, needs deliverance. But who will conduct the deliverance? Certainly not a compromised Church. Amidst the turmoil caused by the sexual revolution, the Church has been embroiled in controversies over doctrinal and historical matters.

Freedom of religion, which is a freedom in America guaranteed by the U.S. Constitution, has enabled denominations to grow and proliferate in the thousands and at alarming speeds. Some have posited that this development has resulted in more of the Americanization of Christianity than in the Christianization of America. There is a need to evaluate many of these denominations to examine what purpose they serve, if any, in light of Scripture.

Denominations and Scripture

> I therefore, the prisoner of the Lord, beseech you that ye walk worthy of the vocation wherewith ye are called, [2] With all lowliness and meekness, with longsuffering, forbearing one another in love; [3] Endeavoring to keep the unity of the Spirit in the bond of peace. [4] There is one body, and one Spirit, even as ye are called in one hope of your calling; [5] One Lord, one faith, one baptism, [6] One God and Father of all, who is above all, and through all, and in you all. (Ephesians 4:1-6, KJV).

The Scripture above talks about maintaining the unity of the Spirit and proclaims that there is one body, one Spirit, one Lord, one faith, one baptism, one God and Father of all. Denominationalism tends to divide up the body of Christ and it has led to a lack of coordination and cooperation in the body of Christ. The splitting of the Church into thousands of denominations gives the impression that the Church consists of associations (churches) founded by the will of her members. It also sometimes gives the impression of a bride at war with herself. The bride must get herself ready and put her house in order for the anticipated return of the bridegroom. The house of the bride cannot be scattered. The bride cannot be divided. Two cannot walk together except they agree. (Amos 3:3). The denominations that profess Christ as Lord and Savior must seek ways to walk together on the straight and narrow way.

The evangelical movement of the 18th and 19th century defined itself against Roman Catholicism. How Christian the Roman Catholic Church is does not fall under the purview of this conversation. However, admitting of certain exceptions, a denomination that is defined mainly by what it is opposed to in the body of Christ rather than what it stands for, only serves to perpetuate divisions.

> For as the body is one, and hath many members, and all the members of that one body, being many, are one body: so also is Christ. ¹³ For by one Spirit are we all baptized into one body, whether we be Jews or Gentiles, whether we be bond or free; and have been all made to drink into one Spirit. ¹⁴ For the body is not one member, but many. (1 Corinthians 12:12-14, KJV).

In 1 Corinthians 12, the Bible recognizes the body of Christ as one. Even though the body is one, it has many members. It is important to note that the many members of the one body are not the denominations. The many members are seen in the context of the spiritual gifts mentioned in 1 Corinthians 12. The members of the body are not institutions like the denominations. The members of the body are individuals redeemed, cleansed, forgiven, and saved by Christ.

> Now ye are the body of Christ, and members in particular.
> (1 Corinthians 12:27, KJV).

> Now you are the body of Christ, and members individually.
> (1 Corinthians 12:27, NKJV).

The members with their spiritual gifts are one in Christ and work together to glorify Christ.

Current Trends in Denominationalism

Many of the church denominations are experiencing a steep decline in membership. Many of the big cathedrals that were filled to capacity a few decades ago are now lying fallow and empty. Some of these cathedrals have even been converted to mosques and museums, especially in Europe. Many of the denominations have failed to connect with fast paced societal trends. They have not done so well at cultural adaptation. If we are to fulfill Christ's Great Commission in Matthew 28:19-20 by taking the Gospel to the four corners of the earth, we must be willing to adapt to the various cultures we will encounter. We must also be willing to adapt and engage with the various stages of the cultural shifts in our environments.

> [19] For though I be free from all men, yet have I made myself servant unto all, that I might gain the more. [20] And unto the Jews I became as a Jew, that I might gain the Jews; to them that are under the law, as under the law, that I might gain them that are under the law; [21] To them that are without law, as without law, (being not without law to God, but under the law to Christ,) that I might gain them that are without law. [22] To the weak became I as weak, that I might gain the weak: I am made all things to all men, that I might by all means save some. [23] And this I do for the gospel's sake, that I might be partaker thereof with you. (1 Corinthians 9:19-23, KJV).

In his letter to the church at Corinth, Paul highlights his ability and willingness to adapt to all that he might win some to the cause of Christ. To fulfill the Great Commission by taking the Gospel worldwide, the Church must be prepared to adapt and connect to a changing culture without diluting her message. It is necessary to understand that Christ is not necessarily against cultural expressions. Christ is not against culture. Christ is above culture. In other words, any culture that is at variance with the gospel of Christ should bow to Christ. (Philippians 2:9-11). The younger generation, which has created its own cultural brand, different from anything the world has ever known, now feels disconnected with the traditional orientation of many of these denominations. This disconnect arises from rapid changes in society and the church denominations' inability to adapt to and engage these cultural shifts in a gospel-oriented fashion. While we recognize that the gospel remains the same, we must recognize that times have changed. The Church must embrace change while remaining faithful to Christ. This is where it has been a challenge for several denominations. By their structure, denominations tend to be rigid in their approach to worship and discipleship. Denominations must be focused on the ministry of salvation and redemption, not on the premise of a leader's personal revelation or upon enforcing rules and rituals.

With the rise of mega-churches claiming non-denominational status, there has been a growing cultural shift away from denominationalism. With the mega-churches have come multi-talented choirs, including professional praise and worship singers that have attracted the younger generation. These things have drawn many, especially the youth, away from denominations that have remained the same way they were when they were founded. Non-denominational Christianity consists of churches that pay minimal attention, if any, to the creeds of other Christian denominations. The non-denominational church has no alignment with any specific Protestant denomination. It has grown astronomically owing to its ability to adapt to various modes and forms while holding tight to the substance of the gospel. Unlike the denominations, it has refused to be bound by history. With the widespread religious pluralism in America, especially within Christianity, the multiplicity of choices has weakened the hold of the clergy over their congregations. There is a current trend of congregations drifting toward churches that are not so much as defined by what their co-founders may have organized centuries back. Congregational shifts appear to be going in the direction of churches that are simply, Bible believing. Nowadays, less emphasis is given to anachronistic occurrences that have little relevance to encouraging a faith based community of believers. Denominationalism may actually be a hindrance to evangelism, especially where denominations are entrenched in their denominational identities instead of being entrenched in Christ. A denomination is not the Church. At best, a denomination consists of a number of local churches that assist the Church in carrying out its mission.

As people have become more needs-oriented, they have sought out churches that can meet their needs. On the other hand, the apostolic church of Jesus Christ challenges the people from a needs-orientation towards a service-orientation. People begin to see that it is in their serving that their very needs are met. It is more blessed to give than to receive.

Many of the denominations, being so rigid and not open to the flow of the Holy Spirit, have inadvertently excluded a generation from connecting to Christ under their auspices. Many of these denominations are struggling to keep their doors open while battling conflicts within and without. Within Christendom, there are disagreements among Protestant, Catholic, Evangelical, Pentecostal, Orthodox, and several others. Just among the Protestants, there are over two thousand denominational factions. Who is dividing us? What is dividing us? Would we surrender our egos and come together to honor the Head of the body, our Lord and Savior Jesus Christ? Or will we rather point fingers at each other and claim that our own exegesis is the right interpretation of Scripture?

No doubt, this growing religious pluralism in the USA and elsewhere has negatively affected the cohesiveness of the Church. It has been said that the Protestant Reformation is the father of thousands of denominations. The lack of cooperation among the denominations has made it difficult for "two to put ten thousand to flight." Loyalty to the denomination, rather than loyalty to the cause of Christ, has further impacted the cohesiveness of the Church. In the face of a common enemy, often times, the Church division became apparent as the Church failed to speak with one voice. This was so apparent in the course of slavery, segregation, communism, and apartheid. The desire to find common ground that would enable the Church to speak with one voice gave birth to the ecumenical movement.

The Ecumenical Movement

From the start of the 20th century, stronger voices began to advocate for the pluralized Christian communities to work together for unity. Some suggested the creation of an ecumenical organization similar to the League of Nations (United Nations). After going through two World Wars in the space of thirty years, churches felt vulnerable. Post-World War II saw a polarized world entrenched in an ideological war. After the war, many churches had to deal with the rise of Communism. Christian unity became a necessity for many churches in order for them to survive the onslaught of Communist and totalitarian governments. The motto "United we stand, divided we fall" was never more appropriate. While this unity was desirable and much sought after, yet there still existed suspicion and unforgiveness among the churches. The call for a united front for all churches was met with reluctance and a wait-and-see attitude by many churches. Attempts at building inter-Christian dialogue are often stunted by our theologies and histories.

Ecumenism grew, partly, from the Roman Catholic Church's attempt to reconcile with Protestant denominations that had parted ways with them over issues of theology. The Second Vatican Council (1962–1965) sought a more robust ecumenical cooperation to *"reconcile diversities amidst denominational identities."* Ecumenism seeks to promote worldwide Christian unity, and cooperation. It argues for the building of bridges, not walls. It seeks to reconcile the divisions in Christian beliefs and practices by working towards unifying the denominations. While the desire to work in harmony is commendable, the challenge lies in the fact that the Word of God makes it clear that two cannot walk together except they agree. (Amos 3:3). There are some sharp doctrinal differences and attitudes that have made it difficult for the denominations, and the "non-denominations" to work harmoniously.

The Church, being the salt of the earth, must work in unity to address certain issues facing humanity. Societal decay has descended into alarming proportions. The root cause of the decay is not easily apparent because it is invisible. It is not political or economic as some suggest. It is spiritual. The political maneuverings and economic corruption and unjust exploitation is as a result of man's insatiable appetite for the things of this world. Man's greed, lust, hatred, and his uncontrollable rivalry, are all spiritual in nature. While the symptoms may be political and economic, the root causes are always spiritual. Being that the root cause of society's decay and the failure of man is spiritual, the Church is the only institution on earth that can address this root cause. However, the Church has been tainted with a bad reputation over the centuries and must humble herself and repent of her complicity in many global atrocities. The Church has run into many pitfalls whenever it acted outside the scope of the Word of God. The truth be told, in spite of forgiveness, the Church is yet to heal from its role in slavery, colonialism, anti-Semitism, clergy pedophilia, and white privilege. The Church will find it difficult to serve where it is not trusted. Trust can be built by the Church living out the love of Christ in a lost world.

Things are falling apart. Crime is increasing. The world is fast losing its moral compass. Abortions (the murder of the most vulnerable and most innocent amongst us) have been legalized in many parts of the world. The Western world is leading the way in encouraging and legalizing same-sex marriages. The attention of men has been captured by the god of this world (Satan). Suicides are increasing. Depression is increasing. Many nations are in economic despair. Part of the mandate of the Church is to bring healing to the nations. The nations are sick. The Church, unfortunately, is also sick and in need of healing. The Church can only receive healing when it is spiritually connected to its Head, Jesus Christ.

> I am the vine, ye are the branches: He that abideth in me, and I in him, the same bringeth forth much fruit: for without me ye can do nothing. (John 15:5, KJV).

The ecumenical efforts of the various denominations will not amount to much if Christ is not at the center of it. In an attempt to bridge the gap among the denominations, a World Council of Churches (WCC) was established in 1948. The idea was to bring theologians of different denominational strata to engage with one another and build partnerships rather than engage in the unhealthy spirit of competition. Many of the churches that were not comfortable with the membership and agenda of the WCC formed the World Evangelical Alliance. Thus, the ecumenical movement got a taste of denominationalism in the sense that it could not keep its idea and organization as one.

Proponents of the ecumenical movement have argued that ecumenism is necessary to build unprecedented alliances among the denominations in the body of Christ so as to meet global challenges and benefit the common people. By working across denominational boundaries, the WCC would have to give a little and take a little. Many churches are not willing to streamline their articles of faith in order to fellowship with other denominations that preach, 'another gospel.' That may be a price too high to pay. Because Christians do not share one theology, it remains to be seen how far this ecumenical approach can go. Doctrinal reconciliation between the denominations remains unrealized. Given the history of Christianity, it would be difficult uniting the body of Christ. Only Jesus Christ can do this.

The challenge of reconciling the Christian denominations can simply be illustrated by the rise of the liberal church denominations. A handful of denominations have succumbed to liberalism. Others have remained committed to remaining orthodox. Generally speaking, amongst the thousands of Christian denominations can be said to be four broad categories: Liberals, Conservatives, Rationalists, and Radicals. Attempts to mix these categories, even in the secular, has always met with minimal success. Orthodox Christians have often been in the forefront challenging the spirit of liberalism that crept into the churches. With a fast-changing culture and the rise of liberalism, churches will have to better articulate their positions of faith to show that they cannot co-habit with strange bedfellows. Liberalism has as its core message that God is loving and will not judge sin. Many liberal Christians do not believe that there is a Holy Spirit that convicts of sin. From this, one can even argue that Christianity and Liberalism are two separate and distinct religions. "Liberal Christianity" seeks a Christianity without the atoning Cross. In reaction to this liberal approach to faith has grown conservative-fundamentalist church denominations that tend to be very exclusive, and legalistic. Conservative Christianity tends to be legalistic, and eventually, isolationist in its Christian approach. The rationalists on the other hand, do not take a literal view of the Bible, and assert that truth is determined by reason and factual analysis rather than by dogma. The rationalists tend to be nominal Christians. They identify with Christ but are unwilling to follow Christ where reason is lacking. Then there is a radical Christianity that places strong emphasis on contending for the faith as laid down in the apostles' teaching in the book of Acts, and all of the Holy Scriptures. The radical Christians pay less attention to the forms of godliness that deny the power thereof. They view their existence and mission solely from the lens of Christ. It is in Christ that the radicals live and move and have their being. Unlike the conservative Christian, the radical Christian tends to operate regardless of denominational boundaries. The radicals within the faith are hardly defined by allegiance to Christian forms and traditions. The radicals must exercise caution in order not to be over-zealous. They must guard against having a zeal that is not according to knowledge. The rationalists, on the other hand, maintain their denominations as a matter of tradition but look to their experience, rather than faith, for inspiration. To them, the church is more of a place to maintain Christian fellowship.

Liberalism, as we saw with the Church of England ordaining gay clergy further resulted in additional breaks and fragmentation of the Church. Attempting to bring liberalism and conservative-fundamentalism under one ecumenical umbrella would seem like a wasted effort.

Ecumenical attempts to reconcile the diverse Christian theologies have also created suspicions that certain denominations are pushing their own clandestine agenda of domination. To remain relevant, the ecumenical paradigm has had to transcend from a standpoint of eliminating the differences among the denominations to seeking areas where consensus was attainable. Nonetheless, our differences have remained the white elephant in the room.

The Limitation of Humanistic Solutions

In bringing the Church back to Christ, we must realize that part of the reason for our multiple fragmentations as a body is traceable to our attempts to help God do His work. In trying to help God, we have created our own path and invited God to join us. Sometimes, the unhealthy rivalry among some denominations reminds me of the man that was not in the company of Jesus' disciples who was casting out demons in the name of Jesus. The apostles forbade the man from doing so because he was not in their company. Jesus corrected His disciples and told them not to forbid the man from calling on His name. Jesus made it clear that whoever was not against them was for them. (Mark 9:38-40).

As we fussed over doctrine and other issues, we assumed that in going our separate ways that God came along with us. The critical question to answer is whether it was God that initiated the separation into a denomination in the first place. If the hand of God was responsible for the breaking away, then those that He led were justified in parting ways from the old established order. As new denominations are established, particularly after great revivals, as was the case in Azusa Street, God will require His leaders to make some adjustments. Leaders must not be in the driver's seat telling God what to do. We can learn a few things from some of the notable denominations, especially from those that emerged after the great awakenings and revivals. One thing that they teach is that you cannot stay where you are and go with God. The history of the Church clearly portrays critical turning points where business just could not be continued as usual. Abram could not remain in Haran and become the father of a nation in Canaan. (Genesis 12:1-8). Many of the leaders and founders of credible denominations had to make sacrificial adjustments to see God move through them and establish His divine purpose. This was especially the case when an old established order was standing in the way of God moving in another direction. On the other hand, others may have carved out a denomination from the Church for human reasons or to accommodate a bias or prejudice.

It will be an unguarded risk to assume that the hand of God has not been in the move towards denominations.

> I make known the end from the beginning, from ancient times, what is still to come. I say: My purpose will stand, and I will do all that I please. From the east I summon a bird of prey; from a far-off land, a man to fulfill my purpose. What I have said, that will I bring about; what I have planned, that will I do. (Isaiah 46:10-11, NIV).

God's ways are not our ways. However, we can determine God's ways from His Word. His Word is clear that He is Sovereign and that He will execute what He has ordained. With the proliferation of church denominations, we must look to the Word of God for guidance and be slow to judge. Denominationalism, as stated previously, has hindered the Church from speaking with one voice. The ecumenical approach to uniting the divergent churches amid complexities of doctrine, histories, and orthodoxies sought to put together parties that were not walking in agreement. The unequal yoking has not worked. The question then arises as to whether it is the Holy Spirit working out this ecumenical attempt at uniting the fragmented and bruised body of Christ. Whatever work the Holy Spirit is going to undertake in this initiative, it would be undertaken in consonance with the Word of God. The challenge has always been how believers interpret the Word. Humanistic solutions have not gone much of a distance in addressing the Church's unity. Rather than run ahead of God, it is best that we wait upon Him. In Acts 5, there was contention over the work of the apostles. They were arrested and brought before the Sanhedrin. Peter defended his faith in Christ and the work he was doing for Jesus Christ. The Sanhedrin were enraged by Peter's testimony and plotted to kill him and the other apostles. Then a member of the Sanhedrin, a Pharisee named Gamaliel cautioned the Sanhedrin. And he said to them: "Men of Israel, take heed to yourselves what you intend to do regarding these men. … keep away from these men and let them alone; for if this plan or this work is of men, it will come to nothing; but if it is of God, you cannot overthrow it – lest you even be found to fight against God." (Acts 5:35, 38-39, KJV). We must adopt a similar approach to denominationalism that has seemed to drive multiple wedges into the body of Christ. Since the bride has failed to fix the problem, it is best to wait for the intervention of the groom. Otherwise, our further taking matters into our own hands may make things worse.

Besides the ecumenical agenda to present all churches as visibly united in Christ, there is a relatively new shift in Christianity going on presently. A growing number of Christians are pursuing Christ but distancing themselves from the Church. They claim to love Jesus but hate the Church. In His message to the church at Ephesus, Jesus Christ commends the church for hating what He hates – the deeds of the Nicolaitans. Jesus also commends some of the churches for loving what He loves. Jesus loves the Church. The Church may not be perfect, but Jesus loves her, nonetheless. The Church is His bride. He died to purchase His bride. To hate or disregard the bride of Christ is to despise Christ. This new trend of churchless Christians might as well become a denomination unto themselves. These brand of Christians are content with knowing Christ without enjoying real fellowship with His body. Many of these churchless Christians are carrying unhealed wounds that they received while in their former churches. Some church leaders may have disappointed them or hurt them and so they abandoned their churches without getting the approval of the Head of the Church, Jesus Christ. A Christian was never designed to be a lone ranger. We must remain in the Church until we see the Church called up to heaven for the marriage supper of the Lamb. (Revelation 19:6-9). The Rapture of the Church will not consider the churches that men have built over the centuries. The Rapture will not consider the church denominations. The Rapture will only discriminate between those that are in Christ and those that are not in Christ.

CHAPTER SIX

LEADERSHIP CHALLENGES

Yet it shall not be so among you; but whoever desires
to become great among you shall be your servant. And
whoever of you desires to be first shall be slave of all.
For even the Son of Man did not come to be served,
but to serve, and to give his life a ransom for many.
Jesus Christ, Mark 10: 43-45, NKJV.

While this book does not focus primarily on leadership, it is crystal clear that the state of affairs in the Church today came about as a result of leadership action, interaction, and lack of action. It will take a depth of leadership to restore the body of Christ to her Christ-appointed position as a bride decked in fine linen, clean and white. It will also take the cooperation of matured leadership working together to see Christ accomplish the reformation of the Church. The Church must come to a place where she can bring in the last harvests before the coming of Christ. There are over six billion souls in need of salvation and the Church must first come back to Christ in order to bring in the harvest. Bringing the Church back to Christ will require church leaders embracing the leading of the Holy Spirit. Bringing in the harvest will require that the Church be prepared for a mass spiritual awakening and revival. We are going to need leaders that hear from God and that are sensitive to the move of the Holy Spirit. To reposition the body of Christ is going to require leadership that is willing to die for the cause of Christ. Where is this quality of leadership to be found?

When God is about to start something new, He raises up a leader. In raising up a leader, God will process that leader to be suitable for the work that is at hand. Men like Abraham, Joseph, Moses, David, Elijah, and Jeremiah were processed in God's fire so that they could be used of God. A mere seminary or Bible college degree, as prestigious as that may be, will not cut it. God seeks leaders in this end times that have been processed in the "Refiner's fire." If they have not been through the fires of testing, then they must be willing to go through the fire. God tested Abraham. (Genesis 22:1). Church leaders that see ministry as a source of comfort are not in a place spiritually to be used by God to bring the Church back to Christ.

The groom is calling for His bride to get ready but where are the leaders that will help prepare the bride for the coming of the groom? What substance are these leaders made of? There is an urgent need to multiply the right godly leadership across board. There is a paucity of leadership for the task at hand. And leaders are not made overnight. Leaders are made by a process. Processes take time, and time is running out.

Biblical Leadership Qualities

In choosing David as king over Israel, God referred to him as a man after His (God's) own heart. God sought a leader that was hungry for God with all his heart. David was such a leader. Christ is the one building His Church. Building often requires construction, re-construction, some demolition, some refurbishing, and some rough work to get the building up to par. In her history, the Church has experienced these building phases. The Church has experienced multiple crisis. In building His Church, we know that Jesus will not accept masking her with beautiful paint when there is still much work to be done. Jesus often spoke against people that painted the outside in order to impress others while the inside was stinking and undesirable. He warned those that had a reputation of being alive and rich but who inside were dead and poor. Jesus is not looking for leaders that are self-seeking, self-promoting, and friends of the world. These kind of leaders only plant and water worldly churches. Churches that are influenced by a spirit of worldliness hardly flow with the Holy Spirit, and are easily hijacked by Satan.

For the spiritual task of bringing the Church back to Himself, Jesus is raising up leaders with certain essential qualities. These qualities are evident in leaders that have been tested in the fire. Such leaders have learnt to gladly deny themselves, take up their Cross, and follow Christ.

1. *Leaders that are anointed by God.* God pays little regard to church leaders that He did not choose. Some are self-appointed just like that woman Jezebel in the church at Thyatira that called herself a prophetess (Revelation 2:20). A leader that God has not chosen and anointed for the purpose of bringing the Church back to Christ will not have the burden to do so. A leader not chosen and anointed by God will have his heart set on other things like a prosperity gospel that has minimal impact on presenting the Church as holy before the Lord. There is an anointing that sets a man apart for leadership. In 2 Kings 9, God sent His prophet to release His anointing upon Jehu. The prophet separated Jehu from his companions and anointed him as king over Israel for the purpose of destroying the house of Ahab and Jezebel. By this anointing only Jehu could accomplish this task for God. In the same way, we must recognize chosen leaders among us that can bring about radical change in the body of Christ. Appointing a novice to a position of leadership or saddling a leader called for a different purpose with the burden of calling the Church together in preparation for Christ's end time visitation (Rapture) will amount to little. Generally speaking, the true apostles in the body of Christ are the ones saddled with the responsibility of spearheading this move of God. It will take an apostolic and prophetic anointing, coupled with intense discipleship, to see the Church restored to its rightful place in Christ.

2. *Leaders that possess the right set of values.* Leaders must be true to the values that they profess. There is no room for hypocrisy in Christ-centered leadership. Christ took a strong stand against the hypocrisy of the Pharisees. Christ will not condone hypocrisy in His leaders. Jesus is not impressed by those that honor Him with their lips while their hearts are far removed from Him. (Matthew 15:8). What we hold with utmost importance and as the core of our life principles is reflected in our values. When Jesus chose His twelve apostles, He did not look for people with class and sophistication. He looked for people that had the right set of values.

These twelve, (with the exception of Judas Iscariot), in spite of their imperfections were totally committed to Christ. They left all to follow Christ. Some left their fathers, some abandoned their nets and their boats to follow Christ. Christ became the very reason, and the singular reason, for their living. While Judas was interested in the money bag, the others were content just being with Christ, their good shepherd. Peter battled with fear (Peter denied Christ thrice), Thomas battled with doubt (would not initially believe the claims of Christ's resurrection), and the other disciples were scattered as soon as their Shepherd was struck. Despite these unfortunate narratives, these disciples possessed the right set of values for the kingdom of God. Jesus invested in their character development. They had godly character. Character is critical to leadership. Character is who the leader really is. Character speaks of integrity. Reputation, on the other hand, is who people perceive the leader to be. Christ worked to train His apostles to have godly character and bear godly fruit. This is the bedrock of discipleship – transforming lives to be Christlike. The apostles were humble men that were teachable. A lack of humility among many church leaders has caused walls to be erected in the body of Christ instead of bridges to be built. Humility is a value. God gives grace to those that embrace this value. Grace is a supernatural empowerment. The leader that operates in humility will enjoy a supernatural enablement from God to do the things required of him.

We need godly leaders that are visionary leaders. The vision must align with Christ's plan and purpose for the Church. Such leaders must have the ability to discern where God is moving and move accordingly. These types of leaders place premium value on possessing a spirit of discernment.

Apostle Gemma Valentine in her book, *Leadership In Motion*, (Page 244) states:

> You'll know a vision is from God when it fits with
> His Scripture; when it furthers His kingdom, and
> when His glory is the chief goal ... When God
> gives a leader a vision to build Him a House, the
> materials he uses in construction will determine
> his reward. The cornerstone of the House of God

cannot be man's philosophy, ideas or opinions, political agendas, the manifesto of anti-Christ governments or doctrines of devils that do not embrace Jesus Christ as Lord. But the wise master builder must use God's Word, God's vision, and plan of reconciliation and redemption as building blocks for kingdom manifestation.

A leader must constantly evaluate his vision in the light of Scripture to ensure that he is not pursuing self-ambition and/or self-glorification. A leader without a vision has no destination in mind and is not working to accomplish a central God-given vision. Such a leader is blind. Leaders that are as blind as a bat, spiritually, will only lead the blind into a ditch. (Matthew 15:14). Leaders must take time to receive training from others that have gone before them or that are ahead of them. Leaders must be constantly learning and seeking knowledge that will advance the cause of Christ.

3. *Leaders that pray.* In these last days, as the day of the Rapture approaches, God is seeking leaders that truly know how to watch and pray. It is going to take a praying Church to access the courts of heaven and bring down the changes needed in the Church. It will require a praying church leadership to lead the churches in prayer. Prayer is important because it is through prayer that we seek the face of God and know His will. Leaders that are not driven to prayer can hardly inspire serious praying in their churches. The importance of prayer can be seen from the value Christ placed on it in His earthly ministry. In Mark 1:35, Jesus rose early in the morning before daylight to pray in a solitary place. In Luke 5:16 we see that Jesus often withdrew into the wilderness to pray. Luke 6:12 records that Jesus prayed all night on a mountain. Jesus, the son of God knew the importance of prayer and did not exempt Himself from prayer. He offered up prayers and supplications with strong crying and tears. (Hebrews 5:7). In Colossians 4:12, Paul makes mention of one Epaphras who labored fervently in prayers for the church at Colossae. Prayer is laborious. It is essential that church leaders lead the way in prayer – praying in the spirit and praying

in their understanding. The offering of mechanical prayers will not move the hand of God or stir God to birth the much talked about revival so desperately needed in our churches today. More prayers are needed for the struggle against principalities and powers, against the rulers of darkness of this world, and against spiritual wickedness in high places. The Church must be fully engaged in spiritual warfare. God is looking for leaders that are ready to war. God is looking for church leaders that are ready to tarry and travail in prayer to see His kingdom come. Leaders that will abandon human strategies learned in human institutions and just bow down before Him.

God often works with a remnant. He has shown time and time again, His preference for quality over quantity. The widow in the New Testament gave the least of the offerings and yet, Christ commended her offering as being of the highest quality. God is looking for leaders with certain qualities and is seldomly impressed by numbers. When it was time for Gideon to raise up fighting men against the Midianites, he raised up a large company of fighting men. God told Gideon that his men were too many.

> ² And the Lord said to Gideon, "The people who *are* with you *are* too many for Me to give the Midianites into their hands, lest Israel claim glory for itself against Me, saying, 'My own hand has saved me.' ³ Now therefore, proclaim in the hearing of the people, saying, 'Whoever *is* fearful and afraid, let him turn and depart at once from Mount Gilead.' " And twenty-two thousand of the people returned, and ten thousand remained. ⁴ But the Lord said to Gideon, "The people *are* still *too* many; bring them down to the water, and I will test them for you there. Then it will be, *that* of whom I say to you, 'This one shall go with you,' the same shall go with you; and of whomever I say to you, 'This one shall not go with you,' the same shall not go." ⁵ So he brought the people down to the water. And the Lord said to Gideon, "Everyone who laps from the water with his tongue, as a

dog laps, you shall set apart by himself; likewise everyone who gets down on his knees to drink." [6] And the number of those who lapped, *putting their hand to their mouth*, was three hundred men; but all the rest of the people got down on their knees to drink water. [7] Then the Lord said to Gideon, "By the three hundred men who lapped I will save you, and deliver the Midianites into your hand. Let all the *other* people go, every man to his place." [8] (Judges 7:2-8, NKJV).

God desires leaders that are prepared for the war. God helped Gideon separate the fighting men by taking them down to the water to be tested. God seeks leaders that can pass the test. Not all church leaders have the vision for this spiritual warfare that must be undertaken on behalf of the Church. Some of the leaders get down to the water and stoop down on their knees to drink instead of lapping from the water with their tongues, as a dog laps. These type of leaders are the ones that want to analyze and debate every move of God. They will do everything but pray steadfastly in the Spirit. They may even point to their human qualifications and yet, are not willing to wage spiritual warfare to uproot demonic hindrances that have stood in the way of Church unity and kingdom advancement for decades.

4. *Leaders that are willing to pay the price.* Leadership has enormous rewards but there is a heavy price to be paid for excellent leadership. Two of Jesus' disciples, James and John, asked Jesus to grant them the right to sit one at His right hand, and the other at His left hand, in heaven. They wanted the perks of leadership. Jesus told them that they did not really know what they were demanding. He asked them, 'can you drink of the cup that I drink of? And be baptized with the baptism that I am baptized with?' Many today desire positions of leadership but have not shown how much of the price they are willing to pay. Those that are going to forge a way for the Church to undergo God's appointed transformation must count the cost and be willing to pay a price above that required of the average believer. To whom much is given, much is required. God's

leaders will face an enormous amount of pressure that will come in the form of criticism, fatigue, and an inadequacy of resources. These weights are enough to drive away the faint-hearted. The price of leadership will require tons of self-sacrifice. Many are unwilling to pay this price. Many profess Christ but are not willing to be counted as fools for Christ.

5. *Leaders that do not have the love of money in their hearts.* The love of money is the root of all kinds of evil. (1 Timothy 6:10). The love of money has permeated an integral part of church leadership to the extent that some pastors and other church leaders have been found to manipulate and deceive people into giving them money. This, in turn, has given the Church a bad reputation as a house of money changers. Leaders of the churches play a considerable role in determining how their churches are perceived by their communities. Some leaders are known for using trickery to obtain the trust of their congregation in order to satisfy their untamed appetite for money. These churches will hardly be known as houses of prayer and houses of worship. Many discerning people see through the scheming of these preachers and have stopped following them. It takes the blind to follow the blind. God is looking for leaders that do not owe allegiance to Marmon. It is impossible to serve two masters. (Matthew 6:24). A person who has not been delivered from the love and power of money will always be led by money. Some church leaders have actually truncated the work of God in their hands and started preaching another gospel, the gospel of prosperity. This is the gospel that elevates prosperity above righteousness.

6. *Leaders that can give birth to other leaders.* The time is short. The harvest is plenty, and the laborers are few. Time is not on our side. Time is winding down. Leaders are needed that can multiply leaders. Yet, leaders are not made in a day. Leaders that God will use cannot be developed on a mass scale. God does His work with potential leaders on a one-on-one basis, The making of true leaders takes time. Leaders must be willing to mentor others and share so much with them. A leader that wants to be in the limelight and thus prevent others from growing cannot contribute much to

repositioning the Church to be cohesive in its approach to end time issues. The hallmark of a good leader is evident in his passion to raise up other leaders. A great leader is the one that takes time to raise up a pool of leaders that are capable of succeeding him. Jesus set the example by training His disciples as leaders for three years that were capable of raising up other godly leaders.

These six factors enumerated above are a few of the essential qualities end time church leaders must have to birth change in the body of Christ. As God raises up these kind of leaders, the rest of the body of Christ must be willing to support them. Leaders are often the recipients of criticisms and character assassination. A leader is strengthened when those that are called to follow his leading encourage him by praying for him and seeing to his well-being. In Numbers 12, Miriam and Aaron criticized Moses because he had married an Ethiopian woman. They began to undermine the leadership of Moses by claiming equal status with Moses. They said, 'Has the Lord indeed spoken only through Moses? Has he not spoken through us also?" This saying displeased the Lord and the Lord rebuked Aaron and Miriam. The Lord inflicted Miriam with leprosy. Aaron repented of his sin to Moses (Numbers 12:11). Many in the Church have criticized church leaders "for marrying an Ethiopian wife," for making an innocent mistake, or for falling short in a certain area. They will need to repent and seek forgiveness from God, and from their leader. In Numbers 16, Korah and his people rebelled against the authority of Moses. They accused him of exalting himself above the other Israelites. Their murmuring and rebellion displeased God and God visited them with His wrath. God destroyed them. God does not take lightly to the disrespect of His appointed leaders, even when those leaders are in the wrong. A good example is provided by David: though king Saul was clearly in the wrong, David consistently submitted to king Saul's authority.

The flip side to dishonoring our leaders manifest when we honor them excessively and to the point of idolizing them. God will never tolerate idolatry. In some churches, the pastor and his office have been so exalted to the point that the pastor is placed on the same pedestal as Christ. A pastor is a fallen human being saved by grace. He must not be given the reverence that is only due to God. The apostle John was in awe at the presence of an angel and fell down to worship before the feet of the angel. The angel forbade John from doing so. (Revelation 22:8-9). Satan often attempts to get the believer's attention off Christ, and then place it on man. Modern church culture, in many parts of the world, have created a new creation: the celebrity pastor. The celebrity pastor may even have more followers than Jesus Christ. It will be difficult for a pastor that is only interested in his success and that of his ministry to be used by God to gather together God's people. "Gather my saints together unto me; Those that have made a covenant with me by sacrifice." (Psalm 50:5, KJV). Leaders that have the task of gathering the saints together cannot be caught up in themselves. As leaders, we must jettison self-promotion and go to the Cross daily to die.

Another area where the Church has been weakened is when leaders fall or fail. Many in the Church fail to realize that pastors and other church leaders are not infallible. They are human and imperfect. Their only perfection is in Christ. It is so disheartening to see believers rejoice at the fall of a Christian leader. The leader falls and then some believers shoot arrows at him when he is down. They gossip and malign him further. God watches to see if we are a people that will show mercy and compassion. Otherwise, we may even be worse than the one we are criticizing and mocking. Love covers a multitude of sins. We must learn not to constantly shoot down our leaders or else a time will come when even competent leaders would be reluctant to serve. I am not saying that we should hold our leaders to a lower standard. Actually, the standard for leadership should be much higher. Nonetheless, in their moment of weakness, our leaders should be given the honor that their office deserves. Doing so does not exempt leaders from correction and being subject to discipline. However, it is wise to remember that it might not be your place to rebuke God's appointed leader. (1 Timothy 5:1).

The Five Fold Leadership Offices

Within the Church there are disputes as to whether all of the five-fold ministry offices are still operational. Christians are divided regarding whether the office of apostle and prophet are still operational in light of Scripture. This is quite a serious matter because it means that many do not know who the leaders of the Church are. Many may not recognize leaders that God recognizes; and many may recognize leaders that God does not recognize. It is a confusing arena but then, we must humbly look to the Scripture for guidance. This misunderstanding and division concerning the status of the five-fold ministry has furthered the divide imposed by denominationalism in the Church. If the Church cannot agree on who a leader is, it would be difficult for the Church to agree on other issues.

> ⁸ Wherefore he saith, When he ascended up on high, he led captivity captive, and gave gifts unto men. ⁹ (Now that he ascended, what is it but that he also descended first into the lower parts of the earth? ¹⁰ He that descended is the same also that ascended up far above all heavens, that he might fill all things.) ¹¹ And he gave some, apostles; and some, prophets; and some, evangelists; and some, pastors and teachers; ¹² For the perfecting of the saints, for the work of the ministry, for the edifying of the body of Christ: ¹³ Till we all come in the unity of the faith, and of the knowledge of the Son of God, unto a perfect man, unto the measure of the stature of the fulness of Christ. (Ephesians 4:8-13, KJV).

The Cessationist Christian is of the view that the office gift of apostle and prophet ceased as soon as the entire Bible was written. The cessationists have relied on certain Bible verses and their experiences to support their position.

> Now therefore ye are no more strangers and foreigners, but fellow citizens with the saints, and of the household of God; And are built upon the foundation of the apostles and prophets, Jesus Christ himself being the chief corner stone: (Ephesians 2:19-20, KJV).

The cessationists take Ephesians 2:20 to mean that all we need to know about salvation and sanctification has been given to us by the apostles and prophets and are contained in the Scriptures. I totally agree with this view regarding salvation and sanctification. However my agreeing with this view still allows me to disagree with the view that the office of prophet and apostle are no longer operational. The fact that the apostles and prophets of Biblical times laid the foundation does not mean that other apostles and prophets are called to lay the same foundation. There is so much work to be done and the ministry of apostle and prophet is not restricted to the laying of the foundation of God's house. A set of apostles and prophets were used to lay the foundation. Another set of apostles and prophets are used to do other things at this particular time. Jesus told a parable of a certain man that hired workers at different times of the day to work in his vineyard. At the end of the day, he gave them all the same wage. The earlier workers could be said to have laid the foundation but that does not invalidate the work of subsequent workers. (Matthew 20:1-16).

The cessationists further assert that Paul referred to himself as the last of the apostles (1 Corinthians 15:4-8) and secondly, that when James, the brother of John was killed, he was not replaced. (Acts 12:2).

> [3] For I delivered unto you first of all that which I also received, how that Christ died for our sins according to the scriptures; [4] And that he was buried, and that he rose again the third day according to the scriptures: [5] And that he was seen of Cephas, then of the twelve: [6] After that, he was seen of above five hundred brethren at once; of whom the greater part remain unto this present, but some are fallen asleep. [7] After that, he was seen of James; then of all the apostles. [8] And last of all he was seen of me also, as of one born out of due time. (1 Corinthians 15:4-8, KJV).

What was Paul saying here? All that Paul was saying here was that he was the last apostle of his time to see the resurrected Christ. He does not make the qualification of an apostle based on physically seeing Christ. He is merely stating that of all the apostles of his time, he was the last to see the resurrected Christ. I have seen the resurrected Christ twice. Jesus Christ has appeared to me twice in my dream. Once in 1992; and subsequently in 2006. A few others like me have also claimed to have seen Jesus either in a dream or a vision. God appeared to Solomon in a dream. He appeared to Moses physically. Moses' experience of God's physical appearance does not in any way, trivialize Solomon's dream experience. In any case as we continue our examination of the Scriptures it will become quite apparent that Paul could not have meant that after him, there were no more apostles. Before we commence a further examination of the cessationist position, it is good that we have a working definition of a modern day apostle and a modern day prophet.

Concerning the *Apostle* and *Prophet* it is important to understand that these titles both relate to the combination of an office and a gift. David Cannistraci, *Apostles and the Emerging Apostolic Movement*, 1996, pg. 29 gives us a definition of an apostle thus: "An apostle is one who is called and sent by Christ to have the spiritual authority, character, gifts and abilities to successfully reach and establish people in Kingdom truth and order, especially through founding and overseeing local churches." An apostle is one sent by Christ to accomplish a particular task. Certainly, the modern day apostle does not do the kind of work the twelve apostles of Jesus Christ did. An apostle is one anointed and sent by Christ for a particular mission. He is commissioned by Christ to not only establish order in local churches but to confront territorial opposition and demonic kingdoms.

> As thou hast *sent* me into the world, even so have I also *sent* them into the world. (John 17:18, KJV).

> But when the fulness of the time was come, God *sent* forth his Son, made of a woman, made under the law, To redeem them that were under the law, that we might receive the adoption of sons. (Galatians 4:4-5, KJV).

> But when the Comforter is come, whom I will *send* unto you from the Father, even the Spirit of truth, which proceedeth from the Father, he shall testify of me. (John 15:26, KJV).

> And when he had called unto him his twelve disciples, he gave them power against unclean spirits, to cast them out, and to heal all manner of sickness and all manner of disease … These twelve Jesus *sent* forth, and commanded them, saying, Go not into the way of the Gentiles, and into any city of the Samaritans enter ye not: But go rather to the lost sheep of the house of Israel. (Matthew 10:1,5-6, KJV).

> (All emphasis in italics are mine).

Apostolic ministry is a "sending" ministry for a particular purpose. From the above, we can see that Jesus was sent by the Father, the Holy

Spirit was sent by Jesus, and the twelve disciples were sent by Jesus. What Jesus was sent to do is different from what the Holy Spirit was sent to do and different from what the twelve apostles were sent to do.

A prophet is one appointed and anointed by God to declare the mind of God in a given situation. Again the cessationist have held that the office of prophet and the gifts of prophecy have ceased. They rely mainly on Hebrews 1:1-2 for their position.

> [1]God, who at sundry times and in divers manners spake in time past unto the fathers by the prophets, [2] Hath in these last days spoken unto us by his Son, whom he hath appointed heir of all things, by whom also he made the worlds. (Hebrews 1:1-2, KJV).

Hebrews 1:1 tells us that in times past, God spoke to us through His prophets. Hebrews 1:2 tells us that in these last days, God has spoken to us by His Son. The cessationists take this to mean that in these last days God no longer speaks. They hold on to the view that God only spoke through His Son. If we are to follow their argument to the most logical conclusion, it will mean that God did not speak again after Jesus ascended to heaven. That would mean that God is not speaking today by the Holy Spirit. That will also mean that God did not speak to the apostles after the ascension of Christ. That will mean that God did not speak to the prophet Agabus in Acts 21. God still speaks today. God can speak to anyone directly, including the vilest of unbelievers. God can also choose to speak through one of His prophets. These are the days of Elijah and the Holy Spirit is establishing, restoring, and driving prophetic ministry in the body of Christ. It is also worthy to note that many cessationists believe that the era of miracles, divine healings, and speaking in tongues have ceased. The office of Prophet is critical in thrusting the Church forward in these last days where it seems that some of the local churches are stuck in a rut. Prophetic voices are being raised in the four corners of the earth to speak a rhema word into the life of the Church. Yet, some cessationists maintain that prophecies are no longer operational because the apostle Paul had stated that prophecies will cease. (1 Corinthians 13:8-10). Again, this is a misinterpretation of Scripture, as Paul was contrasting perfect love with the spiritual gifts. All he was saying is that Love, unlike Prophecy, is eternal. There is no scriptural basis for cessationists' beliefs.

Thankfully, the cessasionists have failed woefully in their attempts to quench the Holy Spirit. They have quenched the Holy Spirit in their congregations and meetings and seek to do same across the body of Christ. The Holy Spirit has been quenched in the cessationists' environment because they hold on to a doctrine that does not give room for the Holy Spirit to show up.

Now let us analyze and rightly divide some Scriptures which negate the cessationist position.

> Wherefore he saith, When he ascended up on high, he led captivity captive, and gave gifts unto men. (Ephesians 4:8, KJV).

In Ephesians 4:8 it is recorded that when Christ ascended up on high, He led captivity captive, and gave gifts unto men. This means that at His ascension, He released gifts unto men. This is referring to gifts given subsequent to His resurrection. In other words, these are ascension gifts. So what gifts did Christ release unto men at His ascension?

> And he gave some, apostles; and some, prophets; and some, evangelists; and some, pastors and teachers. (Ephesians 4:11, KJV).

Ephesians 4:11 lists the office gifts that Christ gave unto men in Ephesians 4:8. Going by the argument of the cessationists, it will stand to reason that if the gifts of apostle and prophet have ceased in the body of Christ then also, must the gifts of evangelists, pastors, and teachers. By the reasoning of the cessationists, it follows that there were only 14 apostles in the entire history of the world: Christ's original 12 apostles, Matthias (replacement for Judas), and the apostle Paul. If there were only 14 apostles, then why did Christ give the gift of apostle to some at His ascension? Who are those "some" He gave the gifts of Apostle and Prophet to? Could Christ have given a gift without a recipient? Let us also bear in mind that Christ is known also by the office of Apostle (Hebrews 3:1). As we continue in our analysis (the rightly dividing) of Scripture, we will find this not to be the case. Jesus appointed the five-fold ministry offices and gifts for a reason. Besides the gifts of God are without repentance.

> 12 For the perfecting of the saints, for the work of the
> ministry, for the edifying of the body of Christ: 13 Till we
> all come in the unity of the faith, and of the knowledge of
> the Son of God, unto a perfect man, unto the measure of
> the stature of the fulness of Christ: 14 That we henceforth
> be no more children, tossed to and fro, and carried about
> with every wind of doctrine, by the sleight of men, and
> cunning craftiness, whereby they lie in wait to deceive.
> (Ephesians 4:12-14, KJV).

Jesus gave the five-fold ministry office gifts at His ascension to strengthen the Church by perfecting the saints for the work of ministry. When all of the five-fold ascension gifts are present in a church, that church is strengthened. That church will have the potential to reach unto the measure of the stature of the fulness of Christ.

Being that Christ called me and consecrated me into the office of Apostle, I owe the body of Christ a duty to humbly explain the nature of my apostolic mandate. A modern-day apostle does not write Scripture as some of the twelve apostles of Christ did. Besides, some of Christ's apostles did not write scripture and may never have even written as epistle. No true apostle on earth today can claim the authority to add or remove from the Scriptures. Apostles today are not called to establish salvation in Christ. Apostles today are called to establish order in the body of Christ and to spearhead the advancing of God's kingdom in the face of opposition from demonic kingdoms. There are other Scriptures from which we can reasonably discern the continuity of the offices of apostle and prophet. Let us go through them briefly to establish the validity of these offices today. In doing so, we will also enter a fuller understanding of what the Holy Spirit is doing in these last days through these offices.

> 28 And God hath set some in the church, first apostles,
> secondarily prophets, thirdly teachers, after that miracles,
> then gifts of healings, helps, governments, diversities of
> tongues. 29 Are all apostles? are all prophets? are all teachers?
> are all workers of miracles? (1 Corinthians 12:28-29, KJV).

What is Paul saying here? Paul here is talking about church organization. He is talking about how God has determined that a church should be organized. The Apostle is first in order, followed by the Prophet. If the Church is to be brought back to Christ, we will need to put our houses in order. Putting our churches in order will mean organizing them according to scripture in the New Testament. Apostles are called by God to establish order in the local churches.

Many heads of Christian denominations are elected by popular ballot or appointed by a church board. They attend an interview for the job of Pastor. End time apostles do not go through such a process. They are often recognized by their local churches as apostles based on their calling and the type and quality of work they do. Often times, God-appointed apostles are refused recognition by many religious denominations. This is not surprising because it is almost impossible for a true apostle to function in a denominational environment.

> [13] For such are false apostles, deceitful workers, transforming themselves into the apostles of Christ. [14] And no marvel; for Satan himself is transformed into an angel of light. [15] Therefore it is no great thing if his ministers also be transformed as the ministers of righteousness; whose end shall be according to their works. (2 Corinthians 11:13-15, KJV).

Again what is the import of Paul's argument in these verses? Paul is giving a warning to the church in Corinth about false apostles that are transforming themselves into apostles of Christ. Why would Paul do this if they were only thirteen apostles with Judas dead and replaced by Matthias and him, Paul? Is Paul insinuating that these false apostles tried to impersonate one of the apostles? I do not think that can be inferred from this narrative. This can only mean that Paul used the word, "apostle" in a generic manner. It is unlikely that he used the word "apostle" here to refer to the twelve apostles of Jesus Christ and himself.

To lay this matter to rest, let us examine one more verse found in Revelation 2.

> I know thy works, and thy labor, and thy patience, and how thou canst not bear them which are evil: and thou hast tried them which say they are apostles, and are not, and hast found them liars. (Revelation 2:2, KJV).

Revelation 2:2 is a part of the message of Jesus Christ given to the apostle John to deliver to the church at Ephesus. These are the words of Christ (written in red letters). The church at Ephesus tested men that claimed to be apostles and found them to be false. If the era of apostles ceased with Paul, the last of the apostles, why would the church in Ephesus bother to be testing to know if these men were apostles? By mere facial recognition, they could have easily known who was and who was not an apostle. It becomes clear that the Ephesian church had to test them to see the authenticity of their apostleship. This would have been unnecessary if the cessationist views held true.

The cessationist fail to see that the term "apostle" is used in Scripture to also mean one specifically delegated by Christ as an ambassador of the gospel. Other apostles in Scripture include Barnabas (Acts 14:4,14) and Andronicus and Junias (Romans 16:7). Paul's reference to being the last of the apostles is made in reference to his time. Paul also calls himself the least of the apostles (1 Corinthians 15:9) relative to his time period.

Denominational structures that do not recognize the five-fold ministry offices hinder believers under their watch from receiving much needed ministry in Christ.

Resolving the Leadership Crisis

Believers hold differing views relating to what value to place on certain offices in the body of Christ. The best way to resolve these conflicts is to go back to the word of God and ask the Holy Spirit to help with our exegesis. Many think they are advancing the cause of Christ, but they may actually be impeding the gospel by not giving their prayers and support to Christians that God has called to lead.

The crisis at hand requires that we be like the church at Ephesus that knew how to test for evil workers and false apostles. We must not throw away the precious baby with the bath water. Thankfully, with the rising irrelevance of rigid denominations that stifle the flow of the Holy Spirit, God has created room in these last days for His apostles and prophets to carry out their assigned mandates. It almost seems as if God is supervising the purging and/or winding down of some church denominations in order to re-position the Church for an enormous end time harvest. The dearth of quality leadership in many of the local churches has meant that the Church has been constrained in fulfilling her divine mission. A cleansing of the Lord's house is much needed. It will take leaders after God's own heart to cooperate with the Holy Spirit in turning the heart of the Church back to her one and only lover that gave His life as a ransom for her: Jesus Christ. We need to seriously examine how much of Christ is in our churches. As we cry out for the Church to be brought back to Christ, we must also cry out for Christ to be brought back into our churches.

CHAPTER SEVEN

BRINGING CHRIST BACK TO THE CHURCH

Even from the days of your fathers ye are gone away
from mine ordinances, and have not kept them. Return
unto me, and I will return unto you saith the Lord of
hosts. But ye said, Wherein shall we return?
Malachi 3:7, KJV.

Bringing Christ back to our churches would mean that we allow the Holy Spirit to have full reign over the governance, structure, and atmosphere of our churches. Christ will come when we are willing to surrender all forms of human control to the Holy Spirit without abdicating our responsibilities. Quite a number of churches claim to have Jesus, but the evidence of His presence is lacking in their midst. Christ has withdrawn from a number of churches and many do not even realize this. The Bible tells of how the Spirit of God departed from Samson without Samson even realizing. (Judges 16:20). While the coming of Jesus Christ may be announced, His departing might not be. In some church settings, the person of the Holy Spirit is hardly ever acknowledged. Jesus Christ promised to send the Holy Spirit. In John 14:18 Jesus said that He will not leave us as orphans and that He will come to us. He fulfilled this promise at Pentecost. (Acts 2). Jesus returned to us by the Holy Spirit. The Holy Spirit is the official helper and comforter of the believer. Those that reject the Holy Spirit are rejecting

Christ (Romans 8:9) and those that deny Christ deny the Father as well. (1 John 2:23). As we seek through prayer, obedience, and warfare to bring the Church back to Christ, we must also seek to bring Christ back to the Church. Like most things in life, bringing Christ back into the Church will require adjustments. Some churches may not even want Christ back in their midst because they are happy the way they are. In the Old Testament, God offered to come and speak with His people. The people told Moses to tell God, "No", because they knew that having God in their midst will require them to make lots of adjustments. They would rather have Moses act as a mediator between God and them. Some churches are like this. They will rather have a substitute for Christ than have Christ in their midst. The problem is that God does not recognize substitutes. God views all substitutes for Him as idols. Many fear that the light of God in their midst will expose their darkness. And this is the condemnation that the light has come into the world, and men loved darkness rather than light, because their deeds were evil. For everyone practicing evil hates the light and does not come to the light, lest his deeds should be exposed. (John 3:19-20, KJV).

Religious traditions have often kept Christ out of many of our local churches. When a church insists on following laid down traditions, especially in their church services, they miss out on what the Holy Spirit wants to do in their midst. Substituting routine and activity for a vibrant relationship with Christ has led to many churches having only a reputation of being alive. These kind of churches might as well be dead. Christ is the vine and we are the branches. A church that is not connected to the true vine has its source of life from another vine. Religious tradition, which is entrenched by a religious spirit, produces dead works. Works, without the unction of the Holy Spirit, no matter how appealing it may seem, are dead works. Many churches must do a self-re-examination to see where they stand with Christ. The Bible admonishes us to examine ourselves to see whether we are in the faith, We must prove our own selves to ensure that Christ is in us and that we are not reprobates. (2 Corinthians 13:5). A willingness to undertake a self-examination is one of the hallmarks of humility. The process of self-examination is a recognition that we may be wrong; and that we are willing to right our wrongs. A people that see no need to go through self-examination will hardly ever question the norms of their traditions and culture. Jesus is Lord over everything including culture and tradition. Every now and then, the Holy Spirit will bring a church to a place where it would have to re-examine some of its orthodoxies and dogmas. A dogma is a principle or set of principles laid down by an authority as absolutely and incontrovertibly true. Nowadays, what merely appears to be true is elevated to a dogmatic status. Hence, the need for us to constantly re-examine ourselves as instructed in the Bible. The Protestant breakaway from the Catholic Church was mainly as a result of the latter church refusing to re-examine its dogmas and orthodoxies. A church is generally classified as orthodox when it strictly conforms to what is traditionally held to be right and true, established, and approved. Martin Luther questioned the beliefs and practices of the Catholic Church in light of Scripture. The result of that questioning gave rise to churches where the Holy Spirit was at liberty to glorify Christ. If we truly desire Christ in our churches, we must make sure that Christ is in all that we say and do.

The church at Laodecia in Revelation 3 had Jesus Christ knocking on their door to enter. Jesus was outside the church. They had kept Him out and He was knocking on their doors to come into their midst. Churches must examine themselves to make sure that Christ is not outside knocking on the door. If He is, we must willingly open the doors for Him to come right in. The problem for some is that Christ is outside knocking on the door, but they refuse to open the door for Him. After a while, their hearts become so desensitized that they cannot hear the knock on the door any longer. Christ is still there. However, their hearts have been hardened to the point where they still carry on the work of the church without the Christ of the Church. Christ will do everything to get such a church's attention. He will send apostles and prophets to bring correction, order, and discipline unto them. It is left for them that have an ear to hear what the Spirit is saying.

> Therefore say to them, 'Thus says the Lord of hosts: "Return to Me," says the Lord of hosts, "and I will return to you," says the Lord of hosts. (Zechariah 1:3, NKJV).

If we want Christ in all of His fulness, in all of His power and glory to return to our churches, we must first begin the process of returning to Him. That process always begins with repentance. When Christ is brought back into the Church in all of His fullness, then His name, His power, and His glory, will be among His people. The Church will be subject to Christ by being obedient to His word and to the leading of the Holy Spirit. Some of our local churches are lacking in power because they are either disconnected or loosely connected to the true vine, Jesus Christ. These churches cannot remain where they are and expect to flow with God.

The Name of Jesus Christ

The name of Jesus Christ must be upon the true Church. When you write your name upon a book or other physical object, it means that you are the owner. The owner's name is usually written upon an object or upon a title deed (for automobiles and real estate properties). So also, the name of Jesus Christ must be over the Church because Jesus Christ, and not man, is the owner of the Church.

> And they shall put my name upon the children of Israel;
> and I will bless them. (Numbers 6:27, KJV).

The name of Jesus Christ conveys His nature. His name conveys who He is and who He is to us. The name of Jesus is awesome. God the Father, Son, and Holy Spirit are One in being, One in essence, One in nature, but not in functionality. For example, Jesus Christ the Son died on the Cross. The Holy Spirit has no blood and so could not be crucified on the Cross. Christ wants His name to be brought back to the churches. He wants to claim the ownership that is rightfully His. Often times, we have used His name without regard to His person. His name must be used in consistency with His nature and His will. The name of Jesus is such a great name and must not be used in vain. It must not be used to swear. It must not be used in carnal language. Christ is grieved especially when His name is used in churches to prophesy lies.

In Acts 3, the apostles Peter and John used the name of Jesus Christ of Nazareth to heal a lame man. They made it clear that the lame man was not receiving his healing from another Jesus but from the Jesus of Nazareth that died on the Cross and that rose from the dead on the third day. At this time, it was common practice to do all things in the name of Caesar. However, the name of Caesar has no power to heal the sick. Today, many churches still rely on the name of Caesar to do God's work. The name of Caesar is a carnal name. A church that does not rely on the name of Jesus for the work of God's kingdom is most likely using the name of 'Caesar'. The name of Caesar comes in various forms such as money, status, influence, and human power. To see Jesus Christ return back to our churches, we believers that make up the Church, must depend on the name of Jesus Christ and on His name alone. Some churches are lukewarm even though they call on the name of Jesus. This is because they have Jesus outside knocking on the door. The name of Jesus changes the atmosphere and makes the church environment conducive for His presence to manifest. Jesus is as close as the mention of His name from the right lips. Many times, the Church calls on the name of Jesus but does not expect Him to show up because faith is not in operation. In an emergency, when we call 911, we expect help right away. In similar fashion, the Church must come to a place that when she calls upon the name of Jesus, she knows that Jesus is working on her entreat.

Others call on the name of Jesus expecting Him to manifest and He does not because they are not in good standing with Him. This was the case with the seven sons of Sceva in Acts 19. Their words were hollow and their attempts to cast out a demon in the name of Jesus Christ resulted in catastrophic consequences being visited upon them. Many times, the name of Jesus has been applied in spiritual warfare and the Church has not tasted the victory perhaps because we have failed to re-examine our relationship with Christ. When Christ sent specific messages to the seven churches of Asia, as recorded in Revelation 2 and 3, He called upon most of them to re-examine their relationship with Him. Some of those churches thought that they were in good standing with Him, but they were not.

In Numbers 6:22-27, God gave instructions to Moses on how the priests were to bless the children of Israel. After the blessing, God said he will cause His name to be put upon them. By putting His name upon them, God was claiming ownership of them. A good name can open certain doors for you in this world, but it cannot open the critical doors of Salvation, Healing, and Deliverance. Only one name can open these critical doors: the name of Jesus Christ. The name of Jesus has no limitation. In heaven and on earth, the name of Jesus Christ has absolute dominion. It is only in the name of Jesus that the Church will accomplish its divine mandate. Many times, churches get so caught up and limited by the name of their denomination. If a work is not being done under the auspices of their denomination, they will hardly recognize it as the work of God. Thus, their denominational name, without their realizing it, begins to take pre-eminence over the name of Christ. The Church must return back to the One that caused His name (ownership) to be placed upon her. The Church, in order to fulfill her end time functions, must allow the name of Jesus Christ to rule and reign in her midst without seeking to control or manipulate the name of Christ. The Church has been given authority by Jesus Christ to operate with signs and wonders. The Church is to do the same works that Christ did, and even, greater works. (John 14:12). Christ has given the Church authority in His name to shake demonic kingdoms and set the captives free. Yet, we are seeing so very few being set free from demonic oppression because many churches have denied the name of Christ. When a church says that divine healing and miracles have ceased in the present dispensation, that church is in essence, denying the name of Christ. Christ has given the Church the keys of the kingdom (Matthew 16:19) and the keys are His name. A key opens and closes. The same thing with the name of Jesus. The name of Jesus binds and loosens. Keys grant access. The name of Jesus grants access to the Church to operate in spiritual realms unknown to the majority of mankind. The name of Jesus opens the door for signs to follow.

> And these signs shall follow them that believe; In my name shall they cast out devils; they shall speak with new tongues; they shall take up serpents; and if they drink any deadly thing, it shall not hurt them; they shall lay hands on the sick, and they shall recover. (Mark 16:17-18, KJV).

From the Bible verses above, it is apparent that the source of the believer's power is found in the name of Jesus Christ. The name of Jesus facilitates a demonstration of God's power. Many churches that are lacking in power tend to have merely a form of godliness that denies the power thereof. The Church exercises power in the name of Jesus because the power belongs to Jesus Christ, and not to the Church. Christ delegated authority and power to believers and to the body of believers (the Church). The believer has power to chase a thousand and the body of believers have power to put tens of thousands to flight.

In Philippians 2, it is recorded that because Jesus made Himself of no reputation and humbled Himself unto death on the Cross, God highly exalted Him and gave Him a name that is above every name. At the name of Jesus, every knee should bow, of things in heaven, and things in earth, and things under the earth. Also, at the name of Jesus, every tongue should confess that Jesus Christ is Lord, to the glory of God the Father. The Bible confirms the superiority of the name of Jesus. This means that the authority in the name of Jesus asserts dominion over every other power. All powers of hell are subject to the name of Jesus. The gates of hell shall not prevail against the Church. The Church must lift up the name of Jesus and refrain and cease from the practice of exalting the name of a pastor or a saint. A church must not be known by the name of her pastor or bishop. A church must be known by the name of God that caused His name to be upon her. Powers opposed to the Church will begin to bow only when the Church applies the name of Jesus in Spirit and in truth.

The word of God demands that the same honor we give to the Father must be given to the Son. That all men should honor the Son, even as they honor the Father. He that honoreth not the Son honoreth not the Father which hath sent Him. (John 5:23, KJV). The status of Jesus demands a reverence for His name. The name of Jesus cannot be taken lightly. The name of Jesus must not be limited by or restricted to man's religious establishments. The Church must invite Jesus in so that His great name can be magnified to the nations.

The Church Should Strive for a New Name

As a result of what Jesus accomplished on the Cross, He was given a name that is above all names. Accomplishments in the spirit realm often results in a change of name. After Abraham's series of faithful encounters with God, his name was changed from Abram to Abraham. Jacob wrestled with the angel of the Lord all night and prevailed. Jacob's name was changed to Israel.

> And he said unto him, What is thy name? and he said, Jacob. And he said, Thy name shall be called no more Jacob, but Israel: for as a prince hast thou power with God and with men, and hast prevailed. (Genesis 32:27-28, KJV).

Jacob's name was changed to Israel because he wrestled with God all night, and prevailed. The Church is overdue for a new name. We are not to be known by such names as deceitful, swindlers, fornicators, money changers, bigots, racist, uncaring, greedy, and scandalous. We are to be known by the names that Christ has named us such as: Body of Christ (Romans 12:4; Ephesians 1:22-23); Bride of Christ (Revelation 19:7); Salt of the Earth (Matthew 5:13); and Temple of the Living God (2 Corinthians 6:16) among many other names.

Often times, at the coronation ceremonies of Monarchs, their names are changed. In the course of slavery, the indigenous names of slaves were changed at the slave auction markets. Babylon was known for changing the names of its captives to Babylonian names. Daniel was given the Babylonian name, Belteshazzar. The three Hebrew young men - Hananiah, Mishael, and Azariah - were given the Babylonian names Shadrach, Meshach, and Abednego, respectively. Also in the spirit realm, our names can be upgraded, and if care is not taken, downgraded as well. Jesus promises the church at Pergamos that if she overcomes, He will give her a white stone with a new name written on it. Today's Church must rise and overcome the stumbling blocks before her, some of which are of its own doing. The Church must be willing to wrestle to enter into her rightful place in Christ Jesus. Just as Jacob wrestled all night, the Church must wrestle for longer nights with the name that has been given to her: the name of Jesus Christ. As the Church honors and exercises the name of Jesus with reverence and in faith, the door is opened for Jesus to come in and move in impossible situations. As Jesus does His glorious work through a sanctified Church, the Church will be known once again in the earth for Righteousness, Peace, and Joy in the Holy Spirit. The name of Jesus must be exalted in the congregation of the righteous.

Faith in Christ

Without faith, it is impossible to please God. (Hebrews 11:6). Some churches have become more of a social club than a house of faith. In some of these churches, the full gospel is hardly preached. Some churches have done away with mentioning the blood of Jesus, claiming that it is offensive to some. Some churches have stopped preaching against sin, claiming that doing so is judgmental. In these churches, essentially liberal churches, the Holy Spirit has departed, and the conviction of sin is absent. Where the Word of God is not preached, faith dissipates. Faith comes by hearing, and hearing comes by the Word of God. (Romans 10:17). Without the preaching of the Word, the Holy Spirit's fire is soon quenched. Faith is exercised through reaching out to God in prayer. Without faith, churches lose their connectivity with Christ. The just shall live by faith. (Romans 1:17). A church that does more of other things and less of preaching the Word and prayer is not a faith based church. Such a church fixes its eyes on what is seen rather than on what is unseen. We are called to live by faith and not by sight. (2 Corinthians 5:7). The eyes of the Church must be fixed not on what is seen, but rather, on what is unseen. (2 Corinthians 4:18). If the life we are living does not demand that we walk in faith, then we are not really following after Christ. When a church rejects the Word of God regarding spiritual gifts such as prophecy and speaking in tongues, then she will have to place her faith on something else. We are not seeing the supernatural power of God working in many of our churches because faith in God's Word is lacking. Many today do not believe that God still heals and delivers.

Some of the church pastors have gotten to the pulpit not necessarily because they were called into that office by Jesus Christ but because they were privileged to get a degree from a Bible College. While graduating from a Bible College is applaudable, it does not necessarily mean that that graduate is called to pastoral ministry. Sometimes, God chooses to use the unlearned to confound the wise. The unlearned may be graced with more faith than the one holding a doctorate degree in divinity. The Church must dethrone head knowledge from being in the driver's seat and let faith lead. Christ will come back to a church that shows that she believes in Him. Head knowledge will perhaps bring Christ to knocking on the door. On the other hand, faith will bring Him in; even faith as small as a mustard seed. It is the lack of faith that has stifled prayer in the churches. Fewer Christians are inclined to attend a prayer meeting and where there is no prayer, the Holy Spirit is absent. It will take the prayer of faith, the effectual and fervent prayer of the righteous to bring Christ back to many churches.

The Power of Jesus Christ

The Church has not operated to her full capacity because there has been a disconnect with the power of Jesus Christ. The Church must come into a fuller awareness of the power that is available unto her in Christ. As churches build much strength in the natural, if not managed properly, this tends to minimize the flow of strength in the supernatural. If you trust in the strength of your natural abilities and connections, then that diminishes your need to rely on God. The Church, especially as an institution, must be reminded of her weakness (sheep among wolves) and therefore, her need to continuously depend on Christ. Our weaknesses are not to be used as an excuse. Rather, the Church must glory in her weaknesses so that God's strength is made perfect in her weaknesses. The enemy is often confounded by the fact that in spite of our weaknesses, we are still standing. As the Church gets to a place spiritually where she sees her weakness, and repents of her pride, the power of Christ will become readily available unto her.

The Acts 2 Church had impact. For our churches to have impact, we must not be spectators. We must not be more interested in ourselves than in the gospel message. We must not be too concerned with our public image to the detriment of the Cross of Jesus Christ. Jesus is the one building His Church and He has sent the Holy Spirit down to the earth to work on every minute detail of the building. The Church is under construction. When Christ is done, we will be like Him.

> Beloved, now we are the sons of God, and it doth not yet appear what we shall be; but we know that, when He shall appear, we shall be like Him; for we shall see Him as He is. (1 John 3:2, KJV).

Christ through the Holy Spirit is building a dynamic Church. This Church is on the move to conquer territory and occupy until Christ returns. The Holy Spirit comes with the power of God to give the Church the empowerment and boost she needs to forcefully advance the kingdom of God. Without God's power it will be impossible to recover lost grounds from the kingdom of darkness. Jesus gave the Church the power she needs to remove demonic hindrances standing in the way of kingdom advancement. Many believers are held captive by demonic powers and strongholds. They have been in the Church for years and yet have not been able to break free from Satan's oppression and entanglement. Though they are stationed in the Church, the power that they need for deliverance remains untapped. Many churches have held on to the lie that a Christian cannot have a demon. As a result, many demonized Christians are suffering with little hope of deliverance. When the power of Christ is trivialized in the churches, the churches lose the opportunity to witness the reality of the kingdom of God. The power of Christ is needed for spiritual warfare and deliverance. Human wisdom and resources are of little consequence in advancing the kingdom of God. While money has its place in advancing the kingdom, money is not the main ingredient for kingdom advancement. Jesus made this clear when He sent out His twelve apostles to transact the business of God's kingdom. They were to heal the sick, cleanse the lepers, raise the dead, and cast out demons. For this particular assignment, Jesus forbade them to take money or other forms of wealth on their journey. Yet, they returned with testimonies of great success. (Matthew 10).

The power of Christ will always fall on an obedient and praying church. Prayer creates an opening for the earthly, physical, natural, visible realm to connect with the heavenly, spiritual, supernatural, invisible realm. The church desiring more of Christ in her midst must return to the place of prayer. Jesus calls His Church a house of prayer. Prayers reminds man of his dependence on God. At the altar of prayer, on bended knees, is where the Church will have to initiate the next battles for kingdom advancement. As the Church moves forward to bring in a global harvest of souls, she is going to need to deploy the power of Christ in large measures. This can only be done through the effectual fervent prayers of the righteous saints. The Church must come together in agreement and pray that, "Thy kingdom come." The kingdom of darkness is on the verge of ushering in a new world order (NWO). The NWO will put platforms in place that will make it easy for the antichrist to easily gain world dominion. The antichrist shall be the sole chief executive of the entire world for 42 months. (Revelation 11:2; Revelation 13:5). The Church must be prepared for fast occurring and rapid changes that will often be driven by demonic forces. The Church must understand the signs of the times and will only get that understanding by revelation. Hence, the need for the spirit of prayer and intercession to return to the churches.

Christ defeated principalities and powers on the Cross and made a public spectacle of them. The church that welcomes Christ in their midst must ensure that the Christ they are receiving is the Christ of the Cross. It is only by the power of the Cross that devils are defeated. Opposition against the Church is becoming intense. The culture of the day is growing in ungodliness. More people are showing interest in things of the occult. Many are turning to the occult to solve their problems. Wizards, witches, and warlocks are trying hard to weaken the Church by populating the churches with their agents. The Church must be very discerning in this hour. The Church must utilize its apostolic and prophetic mantle to launch an all-out war against territorial spirits standing in the way of the gospel reaching all the corners of the earth. Just like the church at Ephesus in Revelation 2 that tested for false apostles, today's churches must do the same. Warfare is desperately needed to stop the spread of religious spirits, and Jezebel spirits in the local church congregations. We cannot afford to keep Jesus knocking on our doors much longer. The Church must confront forces of darkness and overthrow demonic strongholds. Unless the Church engages in spiritual warfare, she will not succeed in dismantling hindrances to the gospel. Churches that operate with an apostolic anointing are well equipped to take down dark territorial rulers in the name of Jesus. The Church will have to go into extended periods of fasting and prayer to see the gospel move. The enemies of the gospel are increasing. However, the Church has been given authority to trample on snakes and scorpions and over all the power of the enemy with the assurance that nothing shall by any means hurt us believers. (Luke 10:19). The Church must exercise her authority in Christ over Satan and his kingdom of darkness.

Satan's devices include deception, temptation, accusation, condemnation, and seduction. The Church must exercise her authority in Christ to set believers free from these wicked devices of Satan. The worst form of bondage is the one where the prisoner does not know he is in bondage. The prisoner not only cooperates with the enemy, he resists being set free. Churches must not get to a place where they are imprisoned by their own rules and traditions without even realizing it. In the words of a famous Russian novelist and journalist of the 19th century, Fyodor Dostoevsky, "The best way to keep a prisoner from escaping is to make sure he never knows he's in prison." The reality is that every church that has kept Christ outside knocking on the door to come in, is in prison.

Christ in His Glory

The glory of God is crying to return to the body of Christ, the Church. The glory does not just want to visit. It wants to remain. It desires to dwell amongst God's people.

In 1 Samuel 4, Israel was smitten in battle by the Philistines. The ark of God which symbolized the presence of God was captured. The grandson of Eli was born at this time and named, Ichabod. "And she named the child Ichabod, saying, The glory is departed from Israel: because the ark of God was taken, and because of her father in law and her husband." (1 Samuel 4:21, KJV). When the presence of God is lacking, His glory cannot come and dwell in the midst of His people. So what we have in several churches is a dry spiritual atmosphere where activity takes place, but God's glory is not seen. Man was made for God's glory and to dwell in the presence of God. God's glory covers His nature, being, essence, will, and power.

Whenever we see God's power transform lives via salvation, healing, and deliverance, His glory is displayed. Man has fallen short of God's glory. Jesus came to restore man into the glory of God that man may glorify God on earth. The church is expected to be a place where the presence of God resides and where God's glory is on display. God is omnipresent but He does not manifest Himself everywhere on the earth. When God's presence is made manifest, His glory is sensed by man. God's glory is often seen in an environment where He is welcomed. When Christ is lifted up, he is glorified. When man is lifted up, man is glorified. God will not share His glory with any man. When man has a visible encounter with the invisible, all powerful, holy God, man gets a taste of His glory. The church must be a place where the glory of God dwells. It must be that when believers gather in the name of Jesus, the glory of God is in the midst of their gathering. The glory cannot come when the Holy Spirit is grieved. The world needs to witness the glory of God. The Church has been given that divine assignment to declare His glory. As we humble ourselves in repentance, Christ who walks among the seven golden lampstands will not only visit our churches with His presence and glory, He will dwell with us as His name, Emmanuel suggests.

CHAPTER EIGHT

REVIVAL

In revival, God is not concerned about filling empty
churches, He is concerned about filling empty hearts.
Leonard Ravenhill

Revival is a spiritual awakening initiated by the Holy Spirit in response to the cries of God's people. Revival is neither birthed by power nor by might. It is birthed entirely by the Spirit of God. Revival is a move of God that leads the people of God to deep repentance of sin and to obedience. For there to be revival on a mass scale, it must begin on an individual level. On an individual level, we must be convicted of sin and broken before God. To arrest the tide of lukewarmness and complacency among many believers, there is an urgent need for us to see our true selves apart from Christ. Self must die on the Cross so that the resurrected Christ can live in us. So often, our self - the flesh - stands in the way of what God seeks to do in our lives and on the earth. Apostasy has visited a significant number of our churches and they have become like that valley of dry bones in Ezekiel 37 that is desperately in need of the Word (flesh and sinews) and the Spirit (the four winds) to revisit them.

Until pastors and church leaders are broken before the Lord in humility and repentance, their call for revival in the body of Christ will continue to fall on deaf ears. Those that God has called into office in the Church must first remove the log in their eyes before they are fit to remove the speck in the eyes of others. The Church is in urgent need of revival, as our Christianity has been polluted by all manner of doctrine that do not carry the weight of conviction of sin. The false prosperity gospel that has been introduced into so many churches hardly encourages brokenness. Brokenness is the process by which our wills are broken to God's will. The prosperity gospel does not preach brokenness. It preaches Christ without the Cross. It mentions the Cross but does not go to the Cross to die. It is an enemy of the Cross of Christ because it places more emphasis on getting material blessings than on becoming Christlike. The prosperity gospel, being a half-baked gospel, cannot usher in the revival that the church so desperately needs. The revival will be birthed through a broken people that tarry before God at the altars of prayer. Revival is not going to come easily. Christians must earnestly want it. Christians must sincerely desire to walk in the light. (1 John 1:6-7). Many Christians have become so nominal in their Christianity. We are called as a chosen generation and not as an apostate generation. There is a cloud of apostasy hovering over many churches. It is in these churches that the cry of revival ought to be loudest. Christ described the church at Sardis as a dead church. They had a reputation of being alive, but they were dead. They were just a step away from apostasy. The church at Laodecia was not dead. It was lukewarm – neither hot nor cold. There are many churches like the church at Sardis and at Laodecia today. Dead in sin, they need to repent of their dead works and walk in holiness.

In bringing the Church back to Christ, it must be emphasized that the Church cannot revive herself. Revival is a renewed life that only dwells in Christ. There are a number of things that allow revival, beginning on an individual level and resulting in a mass revival over our nations and cities.

Ingredients for Revival

The very things necessary for revival are the same things that are necessary to sustain a revival. These things are not only the ingredients for a revival, they are also the evidence and the fruit of a revival. Revival should not be viewed as having an end date. If our lives agree with these ingredients, revival will never cease from us.

1. *Brokenness.* The greatest hindrance to a move of God is not others but, our selves. The old carnal outer man is at war with the new

inner man in Christ. Until the outer man is broken before the Lord, the outer man will keep hindering the inner man, the regenerated spirit from coming forth. The outer man is proud and unwilling to yield. It wants to have his own way all the time and seeks his own glory. Until the outer man is taken to the Cross and crucified, he will continue to dominate the inner man. When the outer man gets to a place where he surrenders his rights to the Lord, then and only then, can he be said to be broken.

> But what things were gain to me, those I counted loss for Christ. Yea doubtless, and I count all things but loss for the excellency of the knowledge of Christ Jesus my Lord: for whom I have suffered the loss of all things, and do count them but dung, that I may win Christ. (Philippians 3:7-8, KJV).

When you are broken, Jesus has all of you and becomes all to you. A broken man is the one that no longer liveth, but has Christ living in him. (Galatians 2:20). So long as self is on the throne, God can hardly flow through you. The life that pleases God is not your life but, the life that you allow Christ to live through you. The alabaster box must be broken.

> And being in Bethany in the house of Simon the leper, as he sat at meat, there came a woman having an alabaster box of ointment of spikenard very precious; and she brake the box, and poured it on his head. (Mark 14:3, KJV).

Until the alabaster box is broken, the precious spikenard will not be released. The life of Christ needs to be released like that precious spikenard. The alabaster box must be broken. The outer man must be broken. The outer man is fond of glorying in his accomplishments and depending on the arm of flesh. Many still place more premium on the alabaster box than they do on the ointment of spikenard. Many still place more premium on their church and what their church is worth than on the life Christ has called them to live. Until we are broken, and the fragrance is released, we are of little use to the Lord. We have this treasure (Holy Spirit, ointment of spikenard) in earthen vessels that the excellency of the power may be of God and not of us. (2 Corinthians 4:7). If the earthen vessel (*the alabaster box*) is not broken, how will the hidden treasure (*ointment of spikenard, costly fragrance, Holy Spirit*) come forth to minister to a dying world? The only place where we can receive brokenness is at the Cross of Christ. The Cross is the altar where our new life in Christ was made manifest. The Cross places a demand on us to die to pride, and to self. We are broken at the Cross. When believers are truly broken, they easily yield to the Word and the Spirit of God. The main purpose of brokenness is not to convict of sin. The main purpose of brokenness is to enable the believer avoid sin. People that are broken do not easily fall for the bait of pride, anger, lust, and other sins. Broken people run away from sin. Broken people flee fornication. Broken people run away from Potiphar's wife and other seducing spirits. The brokenness awaiting the Church will enable her walk in the Spirit, and not fulfill the lost of the flesh any longer. Brokenness stops the flesh from opposing the work of the Spirit.

2. *Repentance*. Sin is what breaks fellowship between the bride and bridegroom. Sin is what breaks fellowship between the believer and Christ. The revival that is long overdue in the Church will burst forth when there is a godly sorrow towards sin that leads to repentance. When we glory in the flesh, this is sin at work. The enthronement of self is sin because its roots are in pride. The Church must repent of all her sin from the past and of her current sin that she may be cleansed in the blood of Jesus Christ. The Church must break the habit of trying to cover up her sinful deeds (e.g. sex abuse among clergy). Covering up sin is not repentance. Covering up sin is walking in darkness. After sinning, rather than come to the light in the cool of the day, Adam and Eve chose to hide from the light. Darkness hates to come before Light. Darkness abhors scrutiny and exposure. Darkness likes to keep things hidden. Darkness thrives where there is no confession and repentance of sin. Thus, if we say that we have fellowship with Him, and walk in darkness, we lie and do not practice the truth. But if we walk in the light as He is in the light, we have fellowship with one another,

and the blood of Jesus Christ His Son cleanses us from all sin. (1 John 1:6-7). The fellowship promised in 1 John 1:7 by our walking in the light is not only fellowship with God but fellowship with one another. Denominationalism has corrupted that fellowship with one another. Denominations tend to see Christians in their particular denomination as better than Christians elsewhere. This does not augur well for fellowship.

Only the blood of Jesus can cleanse us from all sin (1 John 1:6-7) and restore fellowship with God, and with one another. Restored fellowship opens the gates for revival to be birthed in us and around us. Genuine Christian fellowship cuts across denominational lines to the extent that all we see binding us together is the love of Jesus Christ.

3. *Consecration*. A broken person is one that avoids sin. He is in a position to set himself apart unto the Lord. Consecration occurs when you take steps to give yourself unto God. We are responsible for consecrating ourselves unto the Lord. Who then is willing to consecrate himself this day to the Lord? (1 Chronicles 29:5). Consecration is man saying to God, "Here am I. I offer myself up to You as a living sacrifice." When we are consecrated unto the Lord, the Lord then begins to sanctify us by the washing of the Word and by the cleansing of the blood of Jesus Christ. The Church must return to that place of consecration that attracts the refiner's fire to come in and purge the Church of all dead works. A consecrated body of believers (consecrated church) is one that receives an overflow of God's Spirit. The overflow of the Spirit is a hallmark of true revival.

Consecration is an invitation for the Holy Spirit to come and take over. When we consecrate ourselves, we are saying that we desire to take on the nature of Christ the Lamb. The Holy Spirit, symbolized as a dove, always feels welcome to remain on those with the nature of a lamb. (John1:29-34). When churches aggressively embark upon an agenda to be number one in their community, they invariably employ a spirit of competition to accomplish that purpose. Churches are not called to be number one. Churches are called to make Christ number one. There is a difference. Consecration does not admit of carnal methods to accomplish spiritual goals. This is where many followers of Christ missed it in the time of Christ's earthly ministry. They wanted Christ to use carnal methods to show convincingly that he was the Messiah. Christ, thank God, chose to reveal Himself not by man's methods but by the God ordained and prescribed way. Christ accomplished all that He was sent to do because He was consecrated to God the Father. By dying on the Cross and resurrecting from the dead on the third day, Christ clearly and convincingly proved that He is the Messiah.

4. *Prayer.* One of the greatest means to birthing the will of God on earth is through prayer. The Holy Spirit always responds to the fervent prayers of God's people. There has never been a historic revival without extraordinary fervent prayers. Intercessors are needed to birth revival in our churches, communities, and nations. Strong intercessory prayers are needed to tear down and uproot demonic strongholds gripping our cities and towns. God is looking for men and women that will PUSH (Pray Until Something Happens). The Church needs men and women that are focused, consistent, and persistent in prayer. Intercessors that will possess the gates of the enemy are needed so that the enemy is restrained from blocking a much needed revival in this hour. Spirit-filled prayers are in short supply as more churches become lukewarm or remain in a state of spiritual paralysis. William Seymour, a man of fasting and prayer, was used by God to birth the Azusa Street Revival by 1906. The Church must go back to the altar of prayer. Many of our church altars have little or no fire. Many of our altars are known for preaching great sermons. Some prominent pulpits are known for only motivational speeches. Preaching affects men. However, prayer affects God. The preaching of the gospel of Jesus Christ is absolutely necessary. The Word of God is paramount. The Holy Spirit uses the preaching of God's word to convict sinners and bring them to repentance. Faith comes by hearing the word of God. Having received the word of God in faith, we must learn how to wait upon God in prayer and in fasting. Jesus referred to His house as a house of prayer.

I have set watchmen upon thy walls, O Jerusalem, which shall never hold their peace day nor night: ye that make mention of the

Lord, keep not silence, And give him no rest, till he establish, and till he make Jerusalem a praise in the earth. (Isaiah 62:6-7, KJV).

It is important that Christians understand that there is a widespread revival currently taking place in the kingdom of darkness. Satanic forces are becoming more sophisticated and advanced in their means of keeping men in bondage. Wickedness is increasing. The love of men is waxing cold. In this season, the Church must sacrifice her time and resources to gather and develop a company of thoroughbred intercessors that will scatter and destroy mass concentrations of darkness. For the Church to experience the upcoming revival, she will have to continuously engage in spiritual warfare to annihilate principalities and powers standing in the way of this revival.

A church that has gone through and that continuously embraces these four principles mentioned above is a church that is set for revival. Churches that are currently undergoing these experiences must remain focused and wait for God to move. God will make the first move in response to the state of preparedness of the churches.

Mass Revival

The question here is how do we translate the revival of one soul at a time to the revival of our cities and nations? How can revival spread like wildfire? How can we make others experience the very revival, the flooding of our entire being by the Holy Spirit, that we will be experiencing? How do we bring lukewarm Christians aboard the train? How can my personal revival have a domino effect on my community of believers? How can we show other believers what we have become in Christ so that Christ can provoke them to hunger and thirst for a mighty outpouring of His Spirit? If we are simply content with our own personal revival, then we are simply not demonstrating love toward others that are in peril because of their deficiency in the Holy Spirit. Being content with my personal revival while others are lukewarm is a sign of self-centeredness. Fire rekindles fire. When one believer has experienced revival, he must allow himself to be used by the Holy Spirit to ignite a fire in other believers that are asleep. This way, one by one, our churches become alive again. A church that is on fire, pooling her resources together, can reach more people than an individual can. Jesus not only assesses the individual, He assesses our churches. The Church is His bride. The Church must bear fruit, individually and corporately.

Going by the history of ground-breaking revivals such as the Azusa Street Revival in the early 20th century, revivals spread quickly when the church that has received a mighty quickening by the Holy Spirit meets daily in fasting and prayer to cry out for their communities. As more people repent, get saved, and get baptized in the Holy Spirit, demonic strongholds over our cities will begin to yield territory to righteousness.

The Bride and the Harlot

Three women are portrayed in the book of Revelation: The first woman is the woman in Revelation 12 clothed with the sun, with the moon under her feet, and on her head a garland of twelve stars. This woman represents the nation of Israel. Also portrayed in the book of revelation is the bride that gets married to Christ in Revelation 19, and the harlot of Revelation 17. The latter woman is the mother of harlots and of the abominations of the earth who got drunk with the blood of the saints and with the blood of the martyrs of Jesus. God will cause the beast to hate the harlot and destroy the harlot. The beast will have the ability to destroy the harlot, but he will not be able to destroy those that are sealed. (Revelation 7). The beast can destroy the harlot because the harlot is not of God. Christ is not in a relationship with the harlot. What concord hath Christ with Belial? What agreement has the temple of God with idols? (2 Corinthians 6:15-16).

> For a prostitute is a deep pit and a wayward wife is a narrow well. Like a bandit she lies in wait, and multiplies the unfaithful among men (Proverbs 23:27–28, KJV).

> Do you not know that he who unites himself with a prostitute is one with her in body? For it is said, "The two will become one flesh" (1 Corinthians 6:16, KJV).

The bride must not be unequally yoked with the harlot, nor with institutions and persons connected with the harlot. Just like Christ, the Church must be a friend of sinners. However, the Church will require spiritual discernment to know what manner of spirit it is relating to. The harlot is a strange woman. The harlot is the mother of false religion, a one world religion. Whenever the bride gravitates toward the allure of the harlot, like the church in Thyatira did with Jezebel, the church starts to walk in darkness. The religion of the harlot has entered some churches, especially here in America. Yoga and Halloween are celebrated in some so-called churches. Kundalini spirits (serpentine powers) and water spirits have taken over some church altars. Charismatic witchcraft operates today in more than a few churches and is often mislabeled as the power of God. The religion of the strange woman is working hard to defile the bride of Christ. The gates of hell will not prevail against the Church. When the enemy comes in like a flood, the Spirit of God will raise up a standard against the enemy. (Isaiah 59:19). The Holy Spirit works to bring the true bride back to the Cross of Christ: a place of humility, brokenness, conviction of sin, repentance, and holiness.

As previously reiterated, there is a moral deterioration in society that has crept its way also into the churches. It is as if the spirit of the world influences the Church more than the Church influences the world. The ordination of gay clergy and the solemnization of gay marriages, contrary to the Word of God, is now acceptable in some churches. This is the harlot at work – the mother of abominations of the earth. The true bride of Christ must distance herself from these backslidden churches that are blatantly in disobedience to the Word of God. Light has no fellowship with darkness. The bride must distance herself from the harlot.

> Wherefore come out from among them, and be ye separate, saith the Lord, and touch not the unclean thing; and I will receive you. (2 Corinthians 6:17, KJV).

Capturing the Youth

Intercessors and church leaders must work hard to ensure that the youth and young adults get a taste of the revival that is on the way. The youth are the future of the Church on earth and the older generation of Christians must make time and effort to pour into them. The best way to do this is by being an example: certain things are caught rather than taught.

There is a generational shift away from the Church. The Church must be able to relate to and communicate with each generation. Each generation tends to see life differently. In the US, Millennials (1981-1996) and the generation after them have had less contact with organized religion than the generations preceding them. By the time the Millennials came on the scene, religious instruction and prayer had been outlawed in public schools. Christianity is viewed as irrelevant by many Millennials and many churches are on the decline as they have failed to add on a somewhat misunderstood generation to the body of Christ. The Millennials are re-defining the global culture and the Church has struggled to keep abreast with cultural shifts. If the Church does not explore new ways of communication with Millennials, the opportunity to lead a substantial percentage of this generation will be lost. Millennials tend to be technology driven and are quite active on social media. Churches should be very strategic as to their presence on social media. Millennials may not necessarily feel comfortable dealing with the institutionalized church on social media. They seem more at ease dealing with individuals who they can view as mentors. Many millennials tend to be uncomfortable with leaders who flaunt their authority. Many millennials are just seeking for someone that can relate to them and show them the way. Church members, as opposed to the churches, should make a deliberate effort on social media to reach the millennials. After all, Jesus sent out His disciples in twos to reach the people. He never sent out all of them at once to reach the people.

According to Benjamin Windle, "Millennials resist most traditional structures because they were raised in a learning environment that embraced collaboration ... Millennials respond to the relational leader." Benjamin Windle, *8 Innovations to Leading Millennials*. To reach the millennial generation, churches will have to be more intentional with creating a collaborative environment where this generation feel they have an outlet. They need an outlet to be heard, to express themselves without being judged, and an outlet where they can also receive instruction without them feeling it is being shoved down their throats. They also seek an environment where they can be a part of problem solving. In other words, they do not want to be the experiment. They want to be delivered from their challenges and to be taught how to help deliver their peers from similar challenges.

The millennials are the ones best equipped to reach other millennials. This is why churches must make a deliberate effort to disciple the millennials in their ranks. The millennials watch to see if we practice what we preach. When they see the generations before them living a life of faith in the midst of their trials, they are encouraged to do the same. We must keep praying that revival comes to the remnant of millennials that remain in our churches. The millennials, I sense in my spirit, are the ones the Holy Spirit is going to use to spark the flames of revival in our cities and nations. There must be a way to make church more appealing to those that view churches with suspicion because of the many preachers that have given the faith a bad name. Otherwise, Christianity will continue to experience sharper declines. Millennials are the current assets for the future Church. The millennials need to be set on fire for Jesus. We need to focus more on creating the right environment for them to have a sense of belonging. Without watering down the gospel, churches should revisit their approach regarding the needs of millennials. Once the right communication channels are open, and trust is established, we can plant a seed in the heart of the millennials that can spark a fire within their circuits.

Anticipating the Next Big Move of God – The Baptism with Fire

John the Baptist baptized with water. He prophesied that the one coming after him will baptize with the Holy Spirit and fire. These are two separate baptisms from Jesus Christ. The Bible reveals three baptisms. The baptism with water, with the Holy Spirit, and with fire.

> [11] I indeed baptize you with water unto repentance. but he that cometh after me is mightier than I, whose shoes I am not worthy to bear: he shall baptize you with the Holy Ghost, and with fire: [12] Whose fan is in his hand, and he will thoroughly purge his floor, and gather his wheat into the garner; but he will burn up the chaff with unquenchable fire. (Matthew 3:11-12, KJV).

In Matthew 3:12, the gathering of the wheat into the barns is talking of a soul harvest. That soul harvest began in Jerusalem, and in all Judea and

Samaria and is still continuing today to the uttermost part of the earth. The burning up of the chaff with unquenchable fire is what the baptism with fire symbolizes. In Acts 1:5, Jesus tell His disciples to tarry for the baptism of the Holy Spirit. They tarried in prayer and this was fulfilled in Acts 2:1-4. It is recorded in Acts 2:4 that they were all filled with the Holy Spirit. They received the baptism of the Holy Spirit. However, in Acts 2:3, they received what appeared as cloven tongues of fire that sat upon each one of them. In Acts 2:4, they received a baptism, a full immersion of the Holy Spirit. In Acts 2:3, they received what appeared to be divided tongues of fire. They were not immersed in the fire. The fire sat upon each of them. They may not have been baptized with fire here. The baptism of the Holy Spirit was what gave birth to the Church at Pentecost. The baptism of the Holy Spirit in a corporate setting (Acts 2) commenced the Church age as we saw earlier on, especially in Chapter 2. The baptism with fire on a corporate basis appears to be reserved for the end of the church age (closer to the Rapture). Jesus is about to thoroughly purge His floor and gather His wheat into the garner; and then He will burn up the chaff with unquenchable fire. (Matthew 3:12).

> [2] But who may abide the day of his coming? and who shall stand when he appeareth? for he is like a refiner's fire, and like fullers' soap: [3] And he shall sit as a refiner and purifier of silver: and he shall purify the sons of Levi, and purge them as gold and silver, that they may offer unto the Lord an offering in righteousness. (Malachi 3:2-3, KJV).

The fire of the Lord is coming. The book of Malachi mentions two kinds of fire: consuming fire and refiner's fire. Both of these fires come from God and are for two different purposes. The consuming fire of God comes to devour. (Hebrews 12:29). The refiner's fire comes to purify. The fire of the Lord that is about to be poured out on the Church in these very last days is the refiner's fire: the baptism of fire. The fire is not coming to destroy. It is coming to purge the Church of all her issues and get her ready for the Rapture. On an individual level, many have experienced the baptism with fire. However, the next great move of God is a corporate baptism of fire upon the bride of Christ. In Acts 2:4, the Church experienced a corporate (as opposed to an individual) baptism with the Holy Spirit. Now, the Church is about to experience a corporate baptism with fire to purge her and prepare her for the days ahead. The time is short. The bride needs to get prepared to meet the bridegroom. It is going to take the baptism with fire to saturate our churches and prepare her for the Lord's coming. The baptism with fire will bring about a purging and produce holiness in God's people. The baptism with fire does not purge sin. The blood of Jesus is what purges sin. The baptism with fire purges the mind. A renewed mind has no inclination toward sin. The coming baptism with fire will bring transformation to the genuine bride of Christ.

With this coming baptism, our attitude to the cause of the kingdom of God will be in alignment with what the Holy Spirit seeks to do. There will be a renewed zeal for the things of God, especially as world systems continue to fail. The baptism with fire refines and purifies us so that we can have a genuine love for God and for people. This baptism will bring the Church closer to Christ in that the Church will have a renewed zeal for the things of Christ. When the baptism of fire falls upon the Church, the Church will be in a better position to accelerate the agenda of God's kingdom. The baptism with fire removes the fear of man. Without the fear of man, believers would speak boldly about the things pertaining to the kingdom of God.

Also, this baptism with fire will cause the fear of God to return to the Church. In a number of church services, the atmosphere is so casual and shows no reverence toward God. People are on their mobile devices doing other things. People are chatting and eating. In such an atmosphere where there is no reverential fear of God, God will not feel welcome. Here, there could be lots of activities, but the presence of God would be missing. When the fear of the Lord is in the Church, no one will dare offer up a strange fire unto the Lord. When the sons of Aaron offered up a strange fire unto God, God's fire devoured them. Moses then said to Aaron, "This is what the Lord spoke, saying: 'By those who come near Me, I must be regarded as holy; and before all the people, I must be glorified.'" (Leviticus 10:3, KJV). When the baptism of fire falls upon the Church, the Church will give God the glory and the reverential fear that is due to Him. The fear of God enables the presence of God to be in the midst of the Church. The Holy Spirit hardly moves in an environment where God is not esteemed.

The corporate baptism with fire is coming. Just like the corporate baptism with the Holy Spirit that came suddenly in Acts 2:2, the corporate baptism with fire will come suddenly upon the Church as we tarry in prayer. Though it tarry, wait for it for it will surely come!

CHAPTER NINE

TIME IS RUNNING OUT

Watch therefore: for ye know not what hour your Lord
doth come ... Therefore, be ye also ready: for in such
an hour as ye think not the Son of man cometh.
Matthew 24:42, 44, KJV.

Jesus is coming back again for His bride at the Rapture. The Rapture can happen at any time, and the Church must be ready at all times. Christ will come to rapture the Church. He will come as a thief in the night. The timing of the Rapture will be unpredictable and unexpected. The Rapture must be distinguished from the second coming of Jesus Christ. Christ will first draw His Church to Him to meet with Him in the air. The Rapture precedes His second coming to the earth. At the Rapture, Christ does not come down to earth. Rather, He calls up the Church to meet with Him in the air. As the Church awaits Christ, she will not only have to remain prepared but must work in a world where crises will continue to escalate.

It is crucial that the Church is brought into an understanding of the times that we are in. If we lack an understanding of the times, our priorities will be misguided. Time is running out and we must look at the prophetic timeline to understand what has happened, what is happening, and what is about to happen. The Church must be like the men of Isaachar.

> And of the children of Isaachar, which were men that had
> understanding of the times, to know what Israel ought to do;

the heads of them were two hundred; and all their brethren were at their commandment. (1 Chronicles 12:32, KJV).

Because the men of Isaachar understood the times, they knew what Israel needed to do. Understanding of the times is critical. You must be able to distinguish between 'night' and 'day.' Jesus made it clear that He must work the works of the Father while it is day because the night will come when no man can work. (John 9:4). Jesus understood that the night was approaching. So also, the Church must come to an understanding that the night is fast approaching when it will become impossible to work the works of the One that sent her. We do not know the exact time the night will come so we must make maximum use of the day. We cannot afford to waste more time on things that do not impress Jesus. When the night comes, it will not be about work anymore. It will be about survival. (Matthew 24:15-22). While it is still day, there is opportunity for the Church to do the work of the kingdom of God. This is the time for the Church to be a house of prayer that forcefully pushes the agenda of the kingdom of God in the earthly domain. There are so many things of the Kingdom that the Church needs to take by force. Since the days of John the Baptist until now, the kingdom of heaven suffers violence, and the violent take it by force. (Matthew 11:12, KJV). The Bible is not talking of a physical violence. The Bible is talking about a spiritual violence: spiritual warfare.

The signs of the times demand that before the day soon closes and the night opens, the Church must ready herself for some heavy duty spiritual warfare. The spiritual warfare is going to get more intense because the enemy is going to be more empowered in the night. We must weaken the enemy substantially while it is still day. The night speaks of the reign of darkness. As the time for Christ's return fast approaches, the activities of darkness would become more frequent and intense. There will be more wars and rumors of wars, famines, pestilences, and earthquakes in diverse places (Matthew 24) preceding the second coming of Christ. Jesus Christ gave the Church this revelation in order for the Church to be in a state of readiness.

The Rapture

Prior to the second coming of Christ, the event that must take place, (*I am of the pre-tribulation rapture school of thought*), is the Rapture. I remain of the firm conviction that the next major event in God's prophetic timeline is the Rapture. For now, let us begin to appreciate that we are in the time where we are waiting for the arrival of the bridegroom, the King of kings, and the Lord of lords, the One and Only Lord of the Universe, Jesus Christ. While the Church awaits the Rapture, tribulation and persecution will continue on an upward trajectory. The Rapture is an event that occurs when Christ calls up all believers, dead and alive, to meet with Him in the air.

> [13] But I would not have you to be ignorant, brethren, concerning them which are asleep, that ye sorrow not, even as others which have no hope. [14] For if we believe that Jesus died and rose again, even so them also which sleep in Jesus will God bring with him. [15] For this we say unto you by the word of the Lord, that we which are alive and remain unto the coming of the Lord shall not prevent them which are asleep. [16] For the Lord himself shall descend from heaven with a shout, with the voice of the archangel, and with the trump of God: and the dead in Christ shall rise first: [17] Then we which are alive and remain shall be caught up together with them in the clouds, to meet the Lord in the air: and so shall we ever be with the Lord. [18] Wherefore comfort one another with these words. (1 Thessalonians 4:13-18, KJV).

At the Rapture, there shall be a rising of the dead in Christ and we that are alive and remain shall be caught up together with them in the clouds to meet with Christ in the air. This meeting with Christ takes place in the air. Christ does not come down to the earth for the Rapture. Jesus' descent towards the earth will be heralded with a shout, with the voice of the archangel, and with the trump of God. At the Rapture, the true Church of God will from that point on be with Jesus Christ forever. (1 Thessalonians 4:17). This event is different from when Christ comes to earth to terminate the reign of the antichrist. The Church at the moment would be caught unawares by the Rapture. Many will be left behind. Then it will become apparent that the institutional, religious church with all the paraphernalia of an establishment, is not necessarily the same as the Church that Christ calls His bride. The former will be left behind; and the latter will be raptured.

In 1 Corinthians 15:51-52, Paul disclosed and unveiled a mystery to the church at Corinth. In reference to the Rapture, he said that we shall not all sleep, but we shall all be transformed in a moment, in the twinkling of an eye, at the last trumpet. The trumpet shall sound, and the dead shall be raised incorruptible, and we shall be changed.

To avoid confusion, it is important to clarify that there are two phases to Christ's second coming. The first phase is the Rapture which will occur prior to the Great Tribulation. At the Rapture, Christ will descend from heaven with a shout, with the voice of an archangel, and with the trumpet of God. The dead in Christ will rise first. The dead in Christ refers to those believers that died in Christ since the Church began at Pentecost. Then the living in Christ who remain shall be caught up together with them in the clouds. We all in Christ, dead and living, shall meet the Lord in the air and from that point on, we shall always be with the Lord. This is the first phase of Christ's second coming. He does not come to the earth physically. Rather, he calls out His bride to be taken up to meet with Him in the air.

The second phase of Christ's second coming is what in the Bible is seen as the Glorious Appearing (Matthew 24:29-30). The Glorious Appearing occurs after the seven year Great Tribulation (Matthew 24:29; Revelation 19:11-21). At the Glorious Appearing, Christ will judge the nations (Matthew 25) and establish His Millennial Kingdom.

The Parable of the Ten Virgins

The Church has a lesson to learn from the parable of the ten virgins.

> [1]Then shall the kingdom of heaven be likened unto ten virgins, which took their lamps, and went forth to meet the bridegroom. [2] And five of them were wise, and five were foolish. [3] They that were foolish took their lamps, and took no oil with them: [4] But the wise took oil in their vessels with their lamps. [5] While the bridegroom tarried, they all slumbered and slept. [6] And at midnight there was a cry made, Behold, the bridegroom cometh; go ye out to meet him. [7] Then all those virgins arose, and trimmed their lamps. [8] And the foolish said unto the wise, Give us of your oil; for our lamps are gone out. [9] But the wise

answered, saying, Not so; lest there be not enough for us and you: but go ye rather to them that sell, and buy for yourselves. [10] And while they went to buy, the bridegroom came; and they that were ready went in with him to the marriage: and the door was shut. [11] Afterward came also the other virgins, saying, Lord, Lord, open to us. [12] But he answered and said, Verily I say unto you, I know you not. [13] Watch therefore, for ye know neither the day nor the hour wherein the Son of man cometh. (Matthew 25:1-13, KJV).

This parable speaks of the Rapture, and not to the second coming of Christ as some suppose. What distinguished the wise virgins from the foolish virgins was the presence of oil in their lamps. The oil in this parable, is a reference to the Holy Spirit. The five wise virgins had the Spirit of Christ. The five foolish virgins put on a show. They were properly dressed, looked like bona fide brides for the groom but had no oil in their lamps. The bridegroom tarried and they all slumbered and slept.

The Matthew 25:6 Cry. The ten virgins, both wise and foolish, grew tired waiting for the bridegroom that tarried. Matthew 25:6 records that at midnight a cry was made that the bridegroom was coming. This is the cry of revival that will quicken the real bride to be on her feet to meet with Christ. The midnight cry symbolizes a spiritual awakening for the Church. Unfortunately, "at midnight", many will lack oil in their lamps.

And at midnight there was a cry made, behold the bridegroom cometh; go ye out to meet him. (Matthew 25:6, KJV).

This book, *Bringing the Church Back to Christ*, is a midnight cry. The bridegroom is on His way and the Church must make sure she has sufficient oil in her lamp to cover the long haul when the bridegroom is tarrying. The cry in Matthew 25:6 was given to all the virgins, both wise and foolish. The cry demanded that they *"go ye out to meet him."* He was coming toward them but not coming to them. They were to meet Him on the way. The cry was unequivocal. They were to proceed toward the groom. However, the five foolish virgins did not have enough oil for that journey and had to go to the marketplace to buy oil. That journey is the Rapture. The wise virgins, the true Church of Christ will be caught up to meet Christ in the air. The Church of Christ includes the dead in Christ. The foolish virgins would be left behind.

Matthew 25:10 – Only those that were ready were received by the bridegroom. How ready is the body of Christ for this great event?

> And while they went to buy, the bridegroom came; and *they that were ready* went in with him to the marriage: and *the door was shut.* (Matthew 25:10, KJV). (Emphasis in italics, mine).

A time is coming when the door will be shut. The shutting of the door ushers in the night when no man can work. While it is still day, believers must work to ensure that they have the anointing of the Holy Spirit to sustain them even when they fall into a deep slumber and sleep. The door will be shut against those that are not prepared. Christ is using a parable here to warn believers that He will come like that bridegroom when they least expect. True believers must be ready. The Church must be ready. If we do not start preparing now for the bridegroom, then the fate that befell the five foolish virgins will stare at us in the face. God forbid! Better to prepare. Those that are prepared are ready to receive. You cannot be ready if you have not prepared in advance. Those that are not ready - from all the tribes of the earth - will mourn. (Matthew 24:30). They will mourn because they were not ready. They will by this time, now realize the truth but, by then, it would be too late. The door, the opportunity for salvation, would have been shut.

My apprehension is borne out of the general apathy the Church has toward the Rapture. Majority of Christians view the Rapture as a fantasy or have not even heard of it. When it comes to an understanding of the Rapture, many Christians are like those believers in Acts 19 that even never knew that there was the Holy Spirit. Many believers have not been properly educated about the Rapture.

The Rebuilding of the Jewish Temple at Jerusalem

King David sought to build a temple for God. God instructed David to prepare his son, Solomon to build the temple. David was a man of war with so much blood on his hands and so God preferred Solomon to build the temple. King Solomon built the first temple. This temple was destroyed by the forces of Nebuchadnezzar, king of Babylon in 586 B.C. The second temple was built around 516 B.C. and took roughly 46 years to build. In John 2, when Jesus chased out the money changers from the temple, He said: "Destroy this temple, and in three days I will raise it up. Then said the Jews, Forty and six years was this temple in building, and wilt thou rear it up in three days? But Jesus was referring to the temple of his body. (John 2:18-21). This second temple was destroyed by the Romans in A.D.70.

Presently, the temple mount at Jerusalem is occupied by a Muslim mosque, The Dome of the Rock. Biblical prophecy makes it clear that the Jewish temple will be at that site at the second coming of Christ. Presently, the temple mount at Jerusalem is used by Palestinian Moslems. This Islamic Dome of the Rock upon the temple mount at Jerusalem is an abomination in the sight of our Lord Jesus Christ. Since there is no Jewish temple there now, it means that the temple will have to be rebuilt to fulfill the words of Biblical prophecy. Fortunately, Israel took control and possession of the temple site after the Six Day War in 1967. Israel's priests and rabbis are said to be working hard, behind the scenes, to obtain permission to commence the reconstruction of the third temple. The prophet Daniel refers to the third temple at Jerusalem in Daniel 9:27 and Daniel 11:31 when the antichrist defiles the temple with the abomination of desolation. The apostle John also refers to the third temple in Revelation 11:1-2 where an angel commanded him to measure the temple with a reed that was like a measuring rod. Jesus Christ confirmed the thought that a third temple will be rebuilt when in Matthew 24:15 He mentioned the abomination of desolation, spoken of by Daniel, standing in the holy place. The rebuilding of the temple at Jerusalem is evident from many end-time Biblical prophecies of the Great Tribulation. The antichrist will desecrate that temple at the midpoint of the Tribulation. For the antichrist to do so, the temple will first have to be rebuilt. This temple will reactivate the Old Testament style of worship until Jesus Christ comes at the Glorious Appearing to reveal Himself to Israel.

Earnestly Contending for the Faith

In these last days, many religions and false gospels are rising and becoming widespread. Many are being deceived into putting their confidence in a false hope. These are perilous times, and many are desperate for quick fixes to get them out of their hardships. These uncertain times have become the perfect breeding ground for false prophets to thrive and exploit the ignorant. It is at such a time as this that the Church must earnestly contend for the faith. The Christian faith is being attacked, not only by the media, the scientific community, and antichrist religions, but also by certain elements within the institution of the local churches. The true Church must boldly stand up in these last days, before the night cometh when no man can work, and earnestly contend for the faith. There are so many distractions. The Church must remove herself from the distractions and fix her eyes on Jesus, the author, the perfecter, and the finisher of her faith. (Hebrews 12:2).

> Beloved, when I gave all diligence to write unto you of the common salvation, it was needful for me to write unto you, and exhort you that ye should earnestly contend for the faith which was once delivered unto the saints. (Jude 1:3, KJV).

Today, the world continues to question the relevance of the Church. Even many professing Christians have disengaged from the Church and see it as no longer relevant. This unfortunate state of affairs may have its origins in denominationalism which essentially hindered the Church from speaking with one voice. When the Church does not speak with one voice, it becomes difficult to discern what the Church is contending for. If we are just contending to be right, then we are not contending for the faith. Making it more complicated is the fact that Christians are not agreed on what constitutes the Christian faith. And so what one group of Christians are contending for as the faith may be entirely different from what another group is contending for as the faith.

What is the Church earnestly contending for? What should the Church be earnestly contending for?

In Romans 1:28, the Scriptures talk about a people that did not like to retain God in their knowledge. God gave these people over to a reprobate mind that caused them to do things that ought not to be done. There are these kinds of people in Christendom. They have lots of knowledge, but God is not a part of their enormous knowledge base. They do not like to retain God in their knowledge. They are like those Pharisees that search the scriptures, thinking that by merely doing so, they have eternal life. Yet, they cannot see the light of Christ in the scriptures. (John 5:39).

They are full of knowledge but little conviction. God is not retained in our knowledge when He is not the center of our knowledge. Many in the Church must be careful not to fall under the fate of Romans 1:28 and must avoid being given over to a reprobate mind. The only way for us to avoid this is by retaining God in our knowledge. Those local churches that have pushed God to the periphery and made something else their priority for such a lengthy period of time may well be operating with a debased and reprobate mind. When Christians idolize conferences, programs, budgets, auditoriums, projects, building projects, pastors, prophets, apostles, and politicians, they push God aside to the periphery. When Christ is not the driving force of what we do, we begin to contend for other things that are not of the faith. This is why some of our local churches, including some of the big and prominent churches, are caught up in doing things that do not relate to the Kingdom of God. They applaud themselves for their accomplishments even when some of these accomplishments were done without God's hand being in it.

The neglect, and in some cases, failure of the Church to earnestly contend for the faith has been costly. It has resulted in the doors of many local churches being opened to religious spirits. The religious spirit wastes no time in removing the focus of the people off from God. The religious spirit knows how to demonstrate a form of godliness that denies the power thereof. It can operate using the name of Jesus but will not honor the Holy Spirit. Eventually, the religious spirit makes a church substitute the presence of God for mere activities and routine. Believers must be thoroughly discipled in the word of God so that they have a basis for testing such contrary spirits.

Distraction, Delusion, and Deception

As the bride awaits the coming of her groom, and as she earnestly contends for the faith, she must watch and pray. She must avoid all distractions. The distractions of the world have a way of taking our focus away from Christ. A church that is not focused on Christ will soon fall into confusion - or a delusion that it is still on the right path. There is a way that seems right unto a man, but the end thereof is destruction. Simply put, delusion occurs when a lie is viewed as truth in spite of all the evidence pointing to its falsehood. Delusion can easily occur when a denomination bases its entire faith structure on the personal revelation of its leader. Deception closely follows after delusion.

> [9] The coming of the *lawless one* is according to the working of Satan, with all power, signs, and lying wonders, [10] and with all unrighteous deception among those who perish, because they did not receive the love of the truth, that they might be saved. [11] And for this reason God will send them strong delusion, that they should believe the lie, [12] that they all may be condemned who did not believe the truth but had pleasure in unrighteousness. (2 Thessalonians 2:9-12, NKJV).

Whenever the Church had taken her eyes of the Cross of Jesus Christ, the enemy had gained ground that enabled it perpetrate darkness over the world. For certain, the gates of hell will not prevail against the Church. However, if the Church does not stand on her foundation (Jesus Christ), she will often find herself being hindered and obstructed by the gates of hell. The Church is at a point where many of her members are fascinated by signs and lying wonders. Just as mentioned in 2 Thessalonians 2:10, there is an unrighteous deception that has swept over certain parts of the body of Christ. The reason for this is because they did not receive the love of the truth, that they might be saved. What then did they receive? The lusts of their hearts put them in a place where they received a reprobate mind. Many have come into the churches and remained without seeking to know Christ. Many in the visible church are not saved. They attend church services and meetings, but they have not had a personal encounter with the Christ that saves. Many of them in church could be under a strong delusion that hinders them from believing the truth. It is God, not Satan, that gives them over to a strong delusion because they do not have a love for the truth.

The Church must recover back her love for the truth, even unto the death. The bride, just like Christ the groom, must be ready to stand up for the truth without fear or compromise. The Church must not embrace a relative truth as many liberal Christians have advocated. Truth is either the truth or it is not. Truth is absolute. Truth is Jesus Christ. Any truth apart from Christ is a lie. (John 14:6). So why is there not a love of the truth in many of our churches? Why is there such a love for prosperity and other earthly things even at the expense of the truth? The simple answer to these questions is that the truth convicts. They do not love the truth because they take pleasure in unrighteousness. Please bear in mind that unrighteousness includes self-righteousness. When a church begins to base her righteousness on her works rather than the righteousness of Christ, she begins to deviate from truth. This was the issue with the church at Galatia and the Apostle Paul had to rebuke her for deviating from the faith, and trusting in a righteousness that was based on the law. (Galatians 3). The scripture makes it clear that when people refuse to believe the truth because they take pleasure in unrighteousness, God will hand them over to a delusion.

In 2 Chronicles 18, we see how God deals shrewdly with the devious. (Psalm 18:26, NIV). King Ahab of Israel surrounded himself with false prophets. Ahab had no love of the truth and so despised the true prophets of God. The Lord authorized a lying spirit to go and entice king Ahab to his fall in battle. God, however, cannot lie. (Titus 1:2).

> [18] Again he said, Therefore hear the word of the Lord; I saw the Lord sitting upon his throne, and all the host of heaven standing on his right hand and on his left. [19] And the Lord said, Who shall entice Ahab king of Israel, that he may go up and fall at Ramoth-gilead? And one spake saying after this manner, and another saying after that manner. [20] Then there came out a spirit, and stood before the Lord, and said, I will entice him. And the Lord said unto him, Wherewith? [21] And he said, I will go out, and be a lying spirit in the mouth of all his prophets. And the Lord said, Thou shalt entice him, and thou shalt also prevail: go out, and do even so. [22] Now therefore, behold, the Lord hath put a lying spirit in the mouth of these thy prophets, and the Lord hath spoken evil against thee. (2 Chronicles 18:18-22, KJV).

So, God gave king Ahab over to a delusion and he believed a lying spirit and died in battle. The Church must guard against lying spirits. In 1 John 4:1, we are told to test the spirits because many false prophets are in our midst. The Church will need discernment in these last days as wickedness increases. We must be quick to discern and cast out every lying spirit in our churches masquerading as an angel of light.

Now the Spirit speaketh expressly, that in the latter times some shall depart from the faith, giving heed to seducing spirits, and doctrines of devils; ²Speaking lies in hypocrisy; having their conscience seared with a hot iron. (1 Timothy 4:1-2, KJV).

For the time will come when they will not endure sound doctrine, but according to their own desires, because they have itching ears, they will heap up for themselves teachers; and they will turn their ears away from the truth, and be turned aside to fables. (2 Timothy 4:3-4, NKJV).

A lying spirit often follows the majority and the majority often follow a lying spirit. Most times, God's people are a remnant. The fact that the majority take a certain position does not validate that position. A lying spirit condones unrighteousness and will hardly call out unrighteousness for what it is. A lying spirit will make excuses for unrighteousness and will subtly promote unrighteousness in the congregation of the Lord's people. The Church can no longer afford to tolerate or cover up the activities of lying spirits. Catholic priests, for decades, sexually abused boys in their charge and the Catholic governing authorities maintained a silence. Silence in the face of evil encourages evil to spread. This was the case with some of the priests in the Catholic churches. Also, the Pentecostal and Evangelical churches have had their share of sex and financial scandals. These scandals keep festering because a lying spirit is at work. If the Church desires to be taken seriously by the world that she is called to convert to Christ, then she must not be indifferent toward the lying spirits in her ranks and files. The lying spirit is the spirit at work that gives more credence to man's agenda than to honoring Christ.

When the Church Contends for Man's Agenda

¹⁶And they sent out unto him their disciples with the Herodians, saying, Master, we know that thou art true, and teachest the way of God in truth, neither carest thou for any man: for thou regardest not the person of men.¹⁷ Tell us therefore, What thinkest thou? Is it lawful to give

tribute unto Caesar, or not? [18] But Jesus perceived their wickedness, and said, Why tempt ye me, ye hypocrites? [19] Shew me the tribute money. And they brought unto him a penny. [20] And he saith unto them, Whose is this image and superscription? [21] They say unto him, Caesar's. Then saith he unto them, Render therefore unto Caesar the things which are Caesar's; and unto God the things that are God's. [22] When they had heard these words, they marveled, and left him, and went their way. (Matthew 22:16-22, KJV).

Here in Matthew 22:16-22, the Pharisees acknowledged, though with ill intentions, that Jesus was true because He did not regard the status of men. Jesus taught the Pharisees a good lesson. He told them to render unto Caesar the things which are Caesar's; and to render unto God the things which are God's. The Church of God must exercise proper care and discretion in making sure that she does not cast her pearl before swine.

The Church must not be seen as being under the beck and call of any man, be it a man of God, or a man of high status in society. Certain leaders in the Church have given the impression that they contend for the agenda of politicians. James 2:2-3 also admonishes the Church not to regard the status of men. On several occasions the Church has not heeded this admonition. This became more apparent with the 2016 US presidential elections. The Church seemed torn between Donald Trump of the Republican Party and Hilary Clinton of the Democratic Party. Some church leaders began campaigning for politicians instead of contending for the faith. All of a sudden, a number of church leaders found new heroes in Mr. Trump or Ms. Clinton. The gospel of Jesus Christ was abandoned to promote the cause of Caesar. When these partisan church leaders preached the gospel, it was often manipulated to give preference to their candidate. All of a sudden, Republican prophets and Democratic prophets appeared on the scene prophesying victory for their respective candidates. This opened the doors of several churches for all sorts of spirits to enter in. The mainstream evangelical church publicly endorsed Donald Trump. Other Christians, including the more liberal, endorsed Hilary Clinton. It was a bitter and dirty political contest between the two and some influential church leaders got involved in doing dirty work for the politicians. In addition to the divisions in the church body caused by denominationalism, the church leaders by their indiscrete behaviors in endorsing politicians were further fragmenting the Church. Interestingly, as soon as the elections were over, these church leaders switched back to their gospel message of preaching Christ. Our God is not a God that can be switched off and on in this manner. Forces of darkness are fighting hard to get Christians to fight Christians. Politics is one device they are using to do so. Darkness has used racism and white privilege to divide our churches. Now, it is using politics, and economics. Many of the church bodies that took opposing viewpoints at the last US presidential elections in 2016, are yet to reconcile. The sincerity of the hugs and handshakes are doubtful considering the seeds of political discord that have been sown in the body of Christ. In America, we may as well be shifting into newer forms of church denominations: Democratic churches and Republican churches.

The Church cannot, in the same breath, contend for man's agenda and contend earnestly for the faith which was once for all delivered to the saints. It is impossible to serve two masters. By bringing partisan politics into the houses of God, many in the churches have resorted to spirits of accusation, lying spirits, and spirits of worldliness. Some of our influential church leaders have said hurtful and hateful things just to ensure that their preferred candidate got the advantage. Now, because of politics, Christians are calling each other names they never called each other before. These hurtful things are being said because the Church is not earnestly contending for the faith. When the Church continually casts her pearl before swine, she would eventually lose her fragile reputation. Those influential church leaders that have not demonstrated integrity in their dealings with high profile politicians are causing the Church her reputation. God will allow the enemy to diminish the reputation of His people that are not walking in integrity. Lack of integrity will cause God's people their reputation. This is what the Bible says about these types of leaders:

> These are murmurers, complainers, walking after their own lusts; and their mouth speaketh great swelling words, *having men's persons in admiration because of advantage.* (Jude 1:16, KJV). (Emphasis in italics are mine.)

According to Jude 1:16, these men walk after their own lusts. They are driven by their own lustful agendas rather than the agenda of the kingdom of God. They also speak great swelling words. This means that they are boastful and given to exaggeration. Jude 1:16 goes on to say that these kind of men admire the status of certain persons because of the advantage they will get. According to the Bible, this kind of men are mere advantage seekers.

The Church must turn her back on distractions and be about God's kingdom business in these last days. As the Church rediscovers her position in Christ, she will become better equipped to fulfill her divine purpose on earth. There are so many desperate and needy people seeking answers to life's challenges. Many NGOs and non-profit organizations are working hard to eradicate or alleviate poverty, disease, and illiteracy in the world. The Church must not be idle when all hands need to be on deck.

Charity and Philanthropy

[31] When the Son of man shall come in his glory, and all the holy angels with him, then shall he sit upon the throne of his glory: [32] And before him shall be gathered all nations: and he shall separate them one from another, as a shepherd divideth his sheep from the goats: [33] And he shall set the sheep on his right hand, but the goats on the left. [34] Then shall the King say unto them on his right hand, Come, ye blessed of my Father, inherit the kingdom prepared for you from the foundation of the world: [35] For I was an hungered, and ye gave me meat: I was thirsty, and ye gave me drink: I was a stranger, and ye took me in: [36] Naked, and ye clothed me: I was sick, and ye visited me: I was in prison, and ye came unto me. [37] Then shall the righteous answer him, saying, Lord, when saw we thee an hungered, and fed thee? or thirsty, and gave thee drink? [38] When saw we thee a stranger, and took thee in? or naked, and clothed thee? [39] Or when saw we thee sick, or in prison, and came unto thee? [40] And the King shall answer and say unto them, Verily I say unto you, Inasmuch as ye have done it unto one of the least of these my brethren, ye have done it unto me. [41] Then shall he say also unto them on the left hand, Depart from me, ye cursed, into everlasting fire, prepared for the devil and his angels: [42] For I was an hungered, and ye gave

me no meat: I was thirsty, and ye gave me no drink: [43] I was a stranger, and ye took me not in: naked, and ye clothed me not: sick, and in prison, and ye visited me not. [44] Then shall they also answer him, saying, Lord, when saw we thee an hungered, or athirst, or a stranger, or naked, or sick, or in prison, and did not minister unto thee? [45] Then shall he answer them, saying, Verily I say unto you, Inasmuch as ye did it not to one of the least of these, ye did it not to me. [46] And these shall go away into everlasting punishment: but the righteous into life eternal. (Matthew 25:31-46, KJV).

The body of Christ must get more involved in alleviating conditions of poverty within her communities. It is not enough to stay within the four walls of a church and preach the gospel. The Church must make more sacrifices to help the poor. We cannot watch unbelievers sacrifice so much to alleviate poverty and we remain consumed with building the best auditoriums and having the best technologies. In the parable Jesus tells in Matthew 25, those that did nothing for the least of the people were condemned. They were given so much and yet, turned a blind eye to the needs of their fellow man. The Church must examine herself to see if she has been acting like that Levite or that priest in the parable of the good Samaritan. It seemed that the Levite and the priest were so busy with their religious concerns that they could care less for their fellow man that was at the verge of death. It took a non-religious person, a Samaritan to step up and offer practical assistance and hope to a hopeless man.

I do recognize that the Church cannot be expected to play the role of governments. However, to whom much is given, much is required. Churches must come together and work together in unity to touch lives in their communities. Otherwise, the communities will only see them as a social club that meets on Sundays and other days just for themselves. The foundation of our Christian faith is Charity (Love). When churches unite to touch lives in their communities, the impact will be more substantial than a solo effort. Corporations sometimes form alliances to do charitable work in designated communities. The Church can do same. A situation where church leaders are living lives of opulence amidst the many poor in their congregation is cause for concern. Jesus is a friend of the needy and the Church must have the heart of Christ in these last days. If our communities do not see the love of Christ in us, they would be reluctant to receive the gospel message of Jesus Christ from us. The Church cannot simply be broadcasting that Jesus saves and do nothing to save people from starvation, addictions, and injustices.

Charity demands that churches maintain a healthy budget to support the poor in their community. Some churches do this by having a soup kitchen on weekends to give food to the poor. Churches with bigger resources must in addition to keeping money aside for missions, also work on supporting persecuted Christians. With respect to Christians suffering intense persecution solely on account of their faith, the Church must find her voice. The Church must not be mute and must speak with one voice. The Church cannot be neutral in these matters and must begin addressing these matters in an organized manner.

Many village communities in third world countries are short of schools and basic health facilities. The churches in the more affluent countries can assist them by supporting them financially and materially. Whatever we do for the least of these, we are doing for the cause of Christ. The Church will have herself to blame if she slides into irrelevance in her communities. The Church must live out her gospel message by not only winning souls for Christ but by caring for souls.

Possessing Certain Gates of Influence

As the salt of the earth, the Church must as a matter of urgency, through prayer and hard work, penetrate and permeate certain circles of humanity. As good as prayer is, it must be followed by works. The Church cannot afford to isolate herself from the world. If the Church becomes isolated from the world, she will find it difficult to reach the nations for Christ. Prayer will not cover up for the areas where we are slothful. Even though the church is not of this world, the Church is in the world and must ensure that the kingdom of God permeates through the institutions and systems of the world. In doing so, the Church must recognize that she is like sheep among wolves, and so, must be wise as a serpent, and gentle as a dove. (Matthew 10:16). In bringing God's kingdom closer and into these circles, the influence of the Church grows. As Church influence grows, so does her capacity to win more souls for Jesus Christ. Some main circles where Church influence is required to advance the kingdom of God are as follows:

1. *Education.* This is critical because the minds of children and the youth are being captured and shaped by darkness in an organized school system. The Church must pay attention to the teachers that train her children. More Christians must be willing to serve in the school system. I am not advocating for the Church to take over the school system. Otherwise, people become skeptical of our desiring to help. All I am saying is that there is an urgent need for more godly influences in our schools and college campuses. The growing influence of Satan in schools needs to be checked. More and more schools are celebrating more satanic festivals and ceremonies and yet are prohibited from having prayer in school. The kingdom of God needs to be more influential in the area of education.

2. *Media.* The media is a great tool for shaping the viewpoints of the world. The media is the primary channel for instant transmission of information into the minds of people. What is on the airwaves conditions the public mindset. Main media outlets have constantly fed the world's population with anti-Christian and immoral values. The Church should seek to increase its presence in media in order to help change and shape the way the world sees things. This can be done by encouraging Christian youth to study web media, broadcasting, and media production. One of the major wars being fought right now is the war of information. Psychics and new age prophets have increased their presence in media. Deception is growing. The light of the gospel of Jesus Christ must invade and overthrow the darkness and lies in the media. The kingdom of God needs to be more visible in the electronic and print media. The return of Christ is imminent, and the Church urgently needs to get the message out. Media is a strategic outlet.

3. *Business and Finance.* Without finances, it is difficult to gain influence and significance in the business world. The Church must grow her prosperity, not to feed a few fat cows that milk her dry with their ostentatious lifestyles, but to expand her reach to the uttermost parts of the earth. There is also the need to position more faithful Christians in the world of business. Wealthy Christians can easily influence others by living out their Christian values

before them. It was the wealthy followers of Christ that God used to finance His earthly ministry. Joseph of Arimathea, Nicodemus, and Mary Magdalene were known to have funded Jesus' earthly ministry. The Church should encourage more of her members to become entrepreneurs. Christian entrepreneurs can provide opportunities for churches to flourish. This way also, the local churches are better able to meet community needs and disciple people for Christ in their areas of influence. Christ is not pleased when Christians are stingy. Like the parable of talents in Matthew 25 teaches, we must grow our God-given resources to accomplish the greatest good for the Kingdom.

4. *Government.* There is a strong need for godly leaders - leaders that fear God - to be in our decision making. When the ungodly are in power, we see strange laws like the Same Sex Marriage Act being passed. When it goes well with the righteous, the city rejoices; And when the wicked perish, there is jubilation. (Proverbs 11:10). While we do not pray for the wicked amongst us to perish, we must work to terminate their wicked influence.

These are some of the areas where the Church must begin to have a voice in order to expand the scope of her reach. It is only the Church that has the Christ-given mandate to make disciples of all nations. Doing so will require possessing gates that the enemy has held for lengthy periods of time. If the Church must return to Christ, it must seek Christ in the places where He is at work. Christ is at work in our ghettoes and slums. The body of Christ can have more impact in our slum areas by growing an influence in government, business, finance, media, and education. As the Church ministers in these areas, she would also be challenged to grow her capacity to lift people out of poverty and misery.

Evangelism and The Great Commission

As the Church prepares for the Rapture, she must keep busy with doing the primary tasks that Jesus Christ assigned to her. In Matthew 28:19-20, Jesus gives the leaders of the Church what many Bible scholars have termed as The Great Commission.

> And Jesus came and spake unto them, saying, All power is given unto me in heaven and in earth. Go ye therefore, and teach all nations, baptizing them in the name of the Father, and of the Son, and of the Holy Ghost: Teaching them to observe all things whatsoever I have commanded you: and, lo, I am with you always, even unto the end of the world. Amen. (Matthew 28:18-20, KJV).

The main assignment given to the Church by Jesus Christ is to make disciples of all nations. To make disciples of all nations, the Church must truly demonstrate that she is submitted to discipleship under Christ. To make disciples of all nations, you must first of all be a disciple. A disciple is one that is obedient to the word of Christ and that is led by the Holy Spirit. If the Church is going to make disciples of all nations, she must take the time to understand the nations. The Church must have a better understanding of the nations and their challenges, cultures, and their strongmen. Many churches in these last days will have to make a drastic shift from their focus on self to a focus on the nations. Until we learn to focus on others, we cannot hope to focus on the nations. The Great Commission of Christ challenges the Church to come out of her shell, to leave her four walls, and go to the nations. The Church must become mission driven. The Great Commission is a charge given to the Church to advance God's kingdom. Advancing the kingdom will require that we make some drastic adjustments. The Church must teach the unadulterated word of God to ensure that believers are truly transformed by the renewing of their minds. A renewed mind will not conform to the patterns of the world. The Church cannot afford any longer to be influenced by the cultures of the world. The Church must understand and respect the cultures and traditions of the world in order to advance God's kingdom. The Church must cry out to Christ for a baptism of love for the people of the world. Love speaks volumes to lost souls. Following this, to show our seriousness, church budgets must reflect missions and outreach. In this area, the Church in North America and Europe would have to appreciate that there are now more Christians in Africa, Asia, and South America than there are in North America and Europe. There has been a drastic shift in Christian populations. More churches in Africa and Asia are better positioned to send missionaries to Europe and North America but may lack the financial strength to do so. American churches should consider partnering with churches in other countries without seeking to dominate such a partnership. The Church in America, in spite of her earthly wealth and status, can learn a lot of spiritual lessons from churches in other places.

On earth, America has the largest number of Christian universities, Bible colleges, seminaries, Christian radio, Christian television, Christian magazines, Christian authors, and gospel singers. In spite of these blessings, America has become more ungodly. The Church in America will also do well to allocate a part of her mission budget to soul winning in her community. Souls will not be won for Christ unless we make a conscious, deliberate, and strategic effort to win souls. Salvation of lost people must be a top priority of the Church in these last days.

To be powerful and effective witnesses for the gospel of Jesus Christ, churches that have denied the workings and power of the Holy Spirit will need to humble themselves and repent. Believers in the local churches must be glued to the Cross of Christ. Believers must earnestly seek to be baptized in the Holy Spirit so that they have the ability and power to work for Christ in a hostile world. The Church must learn to depend totally on the Holy Spirit for everything. As the Church works to look outward to the nations, she will come to the place where Christ is – the ripe harvest fields.

Escalation of Crisis

As I write this in May of 2020, the world is going through a major pandemic. The coronavirus (COVID-19) pandemic has shut down most of the world. It has placed citizens of the world in one form of lockdown or other restrictions. Millions have been infected with the virus and hundreds of thousands have died. Thousands are hospitalized and fighting for their dear lives. The pandemic has adversely altered the global economy. At one point, a barrel of crude oil was selling for below $0. Essential items have become scarce. What this foretells for the world economy can only best be imagined. Yet, the Bible warns us in Matthew 24 and elsewhere that more crises are coming. The Church should be prepared for the darker days that may be ahead of her. God has always used periods like these to strengthen the Church. The adversity comes to refine our faith and draw us closer to our Lord Jesus Christ. In the midst of the crisis at hand and other crises that are bound to follow, the Church must operate from a position of strength in order to fulfill her divine mandate. Global financial crisis will compel many churches to revise their budgets. Churches will have to be frugal and at the same time, more generous with their finances.

As crisis escalates, the Church must remain functional. The coronavirus pandemic of 2020 has caused more churches to conduct their kingdom businesses online. More churches subscribed to internet communications and broadcasting services as a result of church building closures. Now, more churches have an online presence and can reach more souls on the internet for Christ. Whatever the devil means for evil, God always has a way to turn it around for the good of those that love God and are called according to His purpose. The church that is Christ-centered will always come out stronger with every passing crisis.

Time is fast running out. Christ is on His way and we must be prepared to meet Him in the air. As the bride prepares for the return of the bridegroom, the bride must occupy until He comes. We are now in those days that Christ, the bridegroom refers to as the days of Noah.

> But as the days of Noah were, so also will the coming of the Son of Man be. For as in the days before the flood, they were eating and drinking, marrying and giving in marriage, until the day that Noah entered the ark, and did not know until the flood came and took them all away, so also will the coming of the Son of Man be. Two men will be in the field: one will be taken and the other left. (Matthew 24:37-40, NKJV).

The true bride of Christ will not be the man left behind in the field. The true bride of Christ will be the one taken. (Matthew 24:40). The false bride will still be in the field, doing the work, when the Rapture takes place. The false bride will be left behind to continue in the field. These are like the days of Noah: regular days where regular things happen in spite of the multiple crises.

God is giving the true bride of Christ the understanding of the times so that we know what we ought to do and how we ought to prepare. We must not be like the foolish virgins. We must not be the one that Jesus will say these words to: "How foolish you are, and how slow of heart to believe all that the prophets have spoken!" (Luke 24:25, NIV).

To learn more about the works of Idemudia Guobadia, visit:

www.overcomersusa.org

YouTube Channel: Warfare Mindset – Apostle ID

https://www.amazon.com/author/idguobadia

Printed in the United States
By Bookmasters